Old Timey Southern Recipes

By

CL Gammon

www.deepreadpress.com

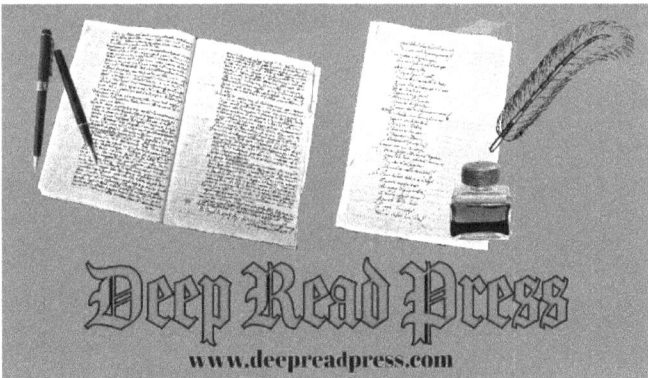

LAFAYETTE, TENNESSEE
deepreadpress@gmail.com

First Deep Read Press Edition.

Published in the United States of America

Edited by: Kim Gammon

Cover Design by: Kim Gammon

ISBN (Paperback): 978-1-954989-37-5

ISBN (Hardback): 978-1-954989-38-2

Published by:
DEEP READ PRESS
Lafayette, Tennessee
www.deepreadpress.com
deepreadpress@gmail.com

Cl Gammon

For Southerners and other food lovers

Contents

Preface

This little volume contains 131 Southern recipes from days gone by. Many of them are still prepared and consumed today. Others are not.

The Southland is a large and remarkably diverse area. The South comprises 14 American states Alabama, Arkansas. Florida, **Georgia,** Kentucky, Louisiana. **Maryland.** Mississippi, Missouri, **North Carolina, South Carolina,** Tennessee, Texas, **Virginia, and the District of** Columbia. Southern cuisine is as diverse as the people residing there. There are recipes unique mostly to the landlocked Midsouth, the Chesapeake area, the Atlantic seaboard, the deep South, Louisiana, and Texas. Other recipes related here are common fare across the South.

This cookbook celebrates the South and it vast array of wonderful food. But no matter what other purposes it may serve, a cookbook should be about food. This cookbook is about food. Make no mistake about that.

Many of the recipes here are more than a century old. Some have been modernized, others have not been. It is up to the chef if he wants to prepare a given dish in a modern appliance or if he wants to use an open fire or a stove that burns wood.

You are encouraged to try these recipes and if you have one or several Southern recipes not provided here, please feel free to email them to the publisher (see the publisher's email address above). If I use your recipe in a later edition, you will receive credit for your contribution.

Bon appétit, y'all.

Introduction

This book uses recipes from olden times. In those days, cooks weren't too concerned about things like calories, cholesterol, or carbs. Nutritional information isn't provided with the recipes presented here. The author leaves it to the individual cooks to find that out for themselves.

Many of the recipes included here call for the use of lard. Of course, the cook may substitute various shortenings or oils for the lard mentioned in the recipes. Additionally, sugar and salt substitutes may be used.

The author makes no claims about the healthiness of these recipes. He only states that they are real and have been used in the past.

There are many ways to prepare a given dish and the author doesn't claim that the recipes mentioned within these pages are the only way to prepare the dishes mentioned. Cooks often add or subtract ingredients and cook things a little harder or softer than other cooks might. A "pinch" or a "dash" to one cook might be different from a pinch or dash to another.

A big part of cooking is trying new things. Don't be tied down by trying to follow these recipes exactly. Follow your dear grandmother's example and experiment with new ingredients.

I. Pork

Southern farm families relied on pork greatly. First, pork was a ready year round source of meat. Swine grew large and were fed from leftover food from farm dinner tables. Pigs were not fussy. They'd eat any "slop" poured into their troughs.

Hogs were called "head to tail" animals because practically the entire animal could be used. Most parts of the animal could be eaten, rendered for lard, or processed into gelatin. The old saying went, "You can use everything from a pig, but its squeal."

Besides feeding farm families, swine was a steady source of income for many of them. Cured hams, ground sausage, and other pork products were sold to neighbors, travelers, and even county stores and the sales were a needed supplement to the other cash crops famers produced.

This chapter lists only 21 of the hundreds of pork recipes used by farmers from years ago. However, they are representative of the ways southerners prepared pork in bygone days, and still prepare it today.

1. Baked Ham

Ham was and is the most popular pork dish. Baked ham is at the top of the list of pork dishes. Below is a simple and easy baked ham recipe.

Ingredients

1 slice ham, 1" thick
½ cup of brown sugar
1 teaspoon of dry mustard
2 cups of milk

Directions

Place the ham in a baking dish. Rub mustard over the top of the ham. Sprinkle it with brown sugar and cover it with milk. Bake it at 300° for one hour.

2. Baked Ham with Apples

There are many ways to bake ham. The recipe below employs apples to make a great dish even better.

Ingredients

2 large, thin slices of raw ham
1 teaspoon of dry mustard
2 teaspoons of vinegar, white
½ cup of brown sugar
1 tablespoon butter
2 apples

Directions

Debone the ham. Mix the mustard and vinegar together. Spread the mustard and vinegar mixture thinly on the ham. Slice the apples very thin and spread them on the ham in 2 layers. Sprinkle the apples with the brown sugar. Roll the ham the long way. Hold it together with metal skewers or tie it with a string. Place it in baking pan and dot it with butter. Bake the ham in a moderately heated oven for 25-30 minutes. Baste several times while baking.

3. Broiled Ham

If one prefers not to bake ham, boiled ham is an alternative. This is an exceptional recipe that is easy to make. This recipe includes raisin sauce (see the recipe in Section IX).

Ingredients

1 slice of ham
1 cup of milk
1 cup of water
Raisin sauce

Directions

Trim all the skin from the ham, and it soak it in 1 cup of water and milk for about 1 hour. Wipe the ham well and place it on a broiler rack. Broil it slowly and when it is cooked fully and slightly browned, remove it from the rack and place it on a hot platter. Serve with raisin sauce.

4. Smithfield Ham

This recipe gets its name from the city in Virgina, not from the pork company. It was once reputed to be the most famous dish to come out of the Old Dominion.

Ingredients

1 ham, 10-12 pounds
2 tablespoons of cracker dust
2 tablespoons of brown sugar
Black pepper
Cloves, whole
Watercress
Parsley

Directions

Soak the ham for twelve hours, then boil it, cooking it very slowly for four to five hours, until it is tender. Cool it in its own essence. When cold, remove the skin and make crisscross gashes in the top of the ham with a sharp knife. Sprinkle two tablespoons of cracker dust, two tablespoons of brown sugar on top of the ham and sprinkle it lightly with black pepper. Stick the ham with whole cloves. Bake it in a hot oven at 450° for 20 minutes until it is brown. Garnish it with watercress and parsley.

5. Ham and Pineapple

At the beginning of the 20th Century pineapple became popular in the United States. It was natural for the good folk of the Southland to create ham and pineapple dishes. Below is 1 terrific ham and pineapple recipe.

Ingredients

1 slice of cured ham 1 inch thick
2 cups of milk
2 tablespoons of butter
1 can of sliced pineapple

Directions

Soak the ham in the milk for four hours. When ready to cook remove ham from the milk and place in hot pan with the butter. Cook slowly until brown and then turn ham and brown on other side. Transfer the ham to another pan and place it in a warm oven where it will stay hot but will not cook. Put slices of pineapple in pan with ham juice and brown on both sides. Then place ham on platter, with slices of browned pineapple on top and around it. Mix the pineapple juice with the ham gravy and pour over the ham.

6. Fried Ham with Red-eye Gravy

Fried ham tastes great, but it may be a little tough and it may need something to soften it a little. That is where red-eye gravy comes in. Red-eye gravy is not really gravy because no flour is used in the recipe. It is made with ham drippings and coffee. Red-eye gravy can be made from salt pork rather than ham, but ham is the usual meat of choice.

Ingredients

1 pound of ham, smoked and cured
Drippings from one pound of fried ham
½ cup of strong black coffee
Crackers

Directions

Fry 1 pound of smoked and cured ham in a skillet. Do not add any other ingredients. Remove the ham but leave the drippings in the skillet. Add ½ cup of strong black coffee to the drippings. Stir constantly and bring the mixture to a boil. Pour the red-eye gravy over ham and crackers.

7. Stuffed Pork Chops

Pork chops are one of the most popular cuts from swine. Below is a delicious stuffed pork chop recipe that is sure to please.

Ingredients

Pork chops
Breadcrumbs
Onions, chopped
Apple, chopped
Water

Directions

Select as many 1" thick pork chops as needed. Make a pocket in each chop. Fill with the following bread filling: 2 cups of breadcrumbs, 1 tablespoon of chopped onion, 1 cup of chopped apples, and season to taste. Use hot water to moisten the stuffing. Place them in a baking dish, add a little water to keep them from sticking. Bake them slowly in an oven until the pork is very well cooked.

8. Roast Pig

Full-grown pigs are often roasted in pits dug into the ground. This recipe calls for roasting a stuffed suckling pig in an oven. For the chestnut dressing, recipe see page XXX.

Ingredients

1 suckling pig
1 red apple
Chestnut filling

Directions

For roast suckling pig use only a very young pig not over six weeks old. Scald the pig by immersing it in hot water (not boiling) for 1 minute. Remove the pig from the water and use a very dull knife to scrape off hair of the pig to keep the skin intact. Then cut a slit from the bottom of the pig's throat to the hind legs and remove the entrails and organs. Wash thoroughly in cold water and chill. Fill the pig with chestnut stuffing and sew the opening together. Roast the pig in an oven 350° for 3-4 hours. When serving, place a red apple in mouth of pig.

9. String Beans and Bacon

Bacon is a mighty popular dish in the South. And not just for breakfast. There are numerous bacon dishes that go well during any meal. The easy to make recipe below combines bacon and garden fresh (or canned) string beans. The results are delicious.

Ingredients

1 can of string beans, or fresh beans
2 medium potatoes (diced into ½" cubes)
¼ pound of bacon, diced and well browned
¼ teaspoon of salt
1 cup of water
Black pepper
1 small onion, whole

Directions

Put all ingredients into a kettle and boil for about 15 minutes until the potatoes are soft.

10. Pigs in Blankets

There are several great Southern dishes called "Pigs in Blankets." This recipe combines bacon and oysters cooked together for a convergence of flavors.

Ingredients

12 large oysters
12 bacon slices
1 pimento
½ teaspoon of salt
Cayenne pepper
Black pepper

Directions

Season oysters with salt and both varieties of pepper. Slice pimento into twelve strips, placing one piece on each oyster. Wrap each oyster with a slice of bacon, closing bacon with a toothpick or skewer. Broil for about eight minutes, browning bacon to a golden brown and crispy brown.

11. Bacon and Kidney Beans

There are several varieties of beans common to Southern recipes. Kidney beans get their turn at bat in this uniquely below the Mason-Dixon line dish. It is a recipe worth making.

Ingredients

2 cans of red kidney beans
½ pound of sliced bacon
1 quart of canned tomatoes
1 teaspoon of baking powder
¼ pound of cheese
Salt
Black pepper

Directions

Cook the bacon crisply, then lift it from the pan. Add the kidney beans to bacon fat. Then tomatoes to which baking powder has been added. Stir it all together. Season to taste with salt and black pepper, put in casserole. Cover closely, set in oven, and cook slowly for 1 hour. Then remove the cover and sprinkle with grated cheese, arrange the bacon strips overall and cook for 10 minutes longer. Serve in the casserole.

12. *Parsnips and Salt Pork*

Salt pork was used extensively in the 19th and early 20th centuries across America, especially in the South. During the Civil War salt pork was a staple of both the Union and Confederate militaries (see the recipe in Section IX). While it is not cooked as often today, the surprisingly versatile product is still used occasionally. The recipe below calls for parsnips. But can be used with many kinds of veggies.

Ingredients

2 pounds of salt pork
6 parsnips
Water

Directions

Cut the salt pork into small pieces, partly cover it with water and cook it until it is almost done. Then add the parsnips, which have been cut into 1" pieces. Cook until both the salt pork and parsnips are tender.

13. Pot Likker

Ingredients

Pot likker (not "liquor") is cooked with another Southern staple – turnip greens. In the 1930s Louisiana Senator. Huey B. Long glorified pot likker as a wonder food. It may not be that, but it is surprisingly flavorful. Corn dodgers (see the recipe in Section IX) are frequently served along with pot likker. The corn dodgers are arranged around the greens.

Ingredients

½ pound slab of salt pork
Turnip greens
Salt
Black pepper
3 quarts of water

Directions

Put a ½ pound piece of salt pork into a pot containing 3 quarts of cold water and boil it for ¾ hour. Put fresh, clean turnip greens into the pot along with the pork and let the mixture boil for 1 hour. Drain the water from the greens and meat. Chop the greens finely and season them well with salt and black pepper. Place the greens on a hot dish and arrange slices of the pork on top of them. Pour 1½ cups of the water in which the greens were cooked (pot likker) over the meat and greens.

14. Pork and Beans

Pork and beans combine salt pork and navy beans for a sweet tasting main or side dish known to every Southerner.

Ingredients

16 ounces of navy beans
¼ pound of salt pork, cubed
1 teaspoon of mustard, yellow
½ teaspoon of salt
Black pepper
1 tablespoon of molasses
½ cup of boiling water
1½ tablespoons of sugar

Directions

If using dried navy beans, cover them with cold water and soak them for at least 12 hours, then change the water, and cook them slightly below the boiling point until their skins burst. To test the beans, take a few and expose them to cold air, if the shells burst, they are done. Drain the beans and add the pork cut into small cubes. Mix the mustard, sugar, salt, black pepper, and water enough to cover the beans. Bake the mixture in the pot slowly for 6 or 7 hours removing pot lid for last hour to brown and crisp the pork.

15. Civil War Fried Salt Pork

If you want an absolutely authentic salt pork recipe from the Civil War, this is it. The recipe for a 1 pound portion of fried salt pork comes from a military manual published in 1861. Rebels and Yankees used the same salt pork recipe.

Ingredients

1 pound of salt pork
Pork fat
1 teaspoon of salt
¼ teaspoon of black pepper
1 pint of water
1 onion, sliced
2 teaspoons of vinegar (if onion is unavailable)
Flour

Directions

Melt some pork fat in a very hot frying pan. Then fry the salt pork in the fat. As the meat is frying, add a teaspoon of salt and ¼ teaspoon of pepper. When the meat is cooked take it out of the pan and set it aside in a dish. Add a pint of water to the remaining fat in the pan along with slices of onion or 2 teaspoons of vinegar. Thicken the mixture with flour to make the gravy. Pour the gravy over the salt pork.

16. Ham Hocks and Pinto Beans

Ham hocks are another item identified strongly with the South. Pinto beans, another Southern favorite, match up beautifully with ham hocks.

Ingredients

2 pounds of pinto beans
1 quart of chicken broth
1 quart of water
1 onion, halved
1 ham hock, cut into halves
1 teaspoon of black pepper,
1 teaspoon of garlic powder
Salt

Directions

Add the beans, chicken broth, water, onion, and ham hocks, to a large pot. Bring the mixture to a boil, then reduce it to a simmer, cover with a lid, and cook it for about 1½ hours. Stir the mixture occasionally, until the beans are nice and tender. Season the dish with black pepper, garlic powder, and salt.

17. Hopping John

Traditionally, Southerners eat black-eyed peas on New Year's Day. Hopping John is a terrific dish to kick off the New Year.

Ingredients

1 cup of cooked rice
2 tablespoons of butter
2 cups of dried black-eyed peas
¼ pound of pork
Salt
Black pepper
Butter

Directions

If using dried black-eyed peas, soak them overnight. The next day, the cook peas until they are soft, being careful to keep them whole during the cooking. Cook the piece of pork with the peas to add flavor. When peas are cooked sufficiently, there should be only a small quantity of liquid left on them. Mix the cooked rice and peas together, season the mixture with salt, black pepper, and butter.

18. Crackling Bread

Cracklings are the pieces of pork skins remaining after the lard has been rendered from the pork. They are available in a variety of stores. While this is a bread dish, it is often eaten as a main course.

Ingredients

1 cup of cracklings (diced)
1½ cups of cornmeal
¾ cup of wheat flour
½ teaspoon of baking soda
¼ teaspoon of salt
1 cup of milk

Directions

Mix and sift the dry ingredients together. Add the milk and stir in the cracklings. Form the mixture into oblong cakes and it place in a greased baking pan. Bake in an oven at 400° for 30 minutes.

19. Pig Feet

There are those that cringe at the thought of eating pig feet. But Southern farmers of old could not afford to waste anything and they found several ways to create tasty pig feet dishes. Below is a simple method for cooking pig feet.

Ingredients

8 pig feet, split
1 onion, chopped
2 celery stalks, chopped
¾ cup of vinegar, white
2 tablespoons of red pepper flakes
2 tablespoons of seasoned salt
1 tablespoon of garlic, chopped
1 teaspoon of black pepper

Directions

Thoroughly wash the pig feet in cold water and place them into a large pot. Add the onion, celery, vinegar, red pepper flakes, seasoned salt, garlic, and black pepper. Pour in water to cover the mixture and then bring it to a boil. Reduce the heat to low and simmer the mixture for about 2 hours until the meat is tender and coming off the bones.

20. Pork Brains and Eggs

The thought of eating pork brains sometimes causes negative reactions. Yet, pork brains are very flavorful and quite nutritious. A common Southern breakfast dish was, and sometimes still is, pork brains and scrambled eggs.

Ingredients

½ cup of lard
2 medium onions, sliced
1 teaspoon of black pepper
1 clove of garlic
2 pork brains, diced roughly
3 eggs, beaten
Salt

Directions

Put the lard into a frying pan and heat it until it is melted. Add the sliced onions and cook them on high heat until they are caramelized. Reduce the heat to medium and add the black pepper and garlic and sauté the mixture for 2-3 minutes. Add the brains to the pan and cook them until the brains take on a white-gray color. Pour the beaten eggs into the pan. Fry the brains and eggs until they are well done. Salt the brains and eggs to taste.

21. Liver, Heart, & Lights Stew

Pork "innards" can be used in a variety of ways, either alone or in combination with each other. This stew combines three internal organs for a hearty dish. Just in case the recipe seems confusing, pork lungs are called "lights." This comes from the fact that pork lungs are not heavy. The British called them lights because of that fact.

Ingredients

Pork liver, heart, lungs (lights)
6 or 7 bacon slices
8 medium potatoes, peeled and quartered
3 celery stalks, cut into 1 inch chunks
2 teaspoons of sage leaves, ground
Salt
Black pepper
1-2 quarts of water

Directions

Cut the liver, heart, and lights into about 1½" cubes, and wash them perfectly clean, being careful to remove any sinewy or gristly fibers. Sprinkle them lightly with salt and black pepper and set them aside. Fry the bacon in a Dutch oven. Remove the bacon and add the celery, onions, and garlic to drippings and sauté the mixture for 2-3 minutes. Add everything but the potatoes to the pot and bring the mixture to a boil, then reduce it to a simmer and cook it for about 1½ hours until liver and lights are fork tender. Check frequently and add additional water as needed. Add the potatoes and let them cook for another 30 minutes. Broth will thicken as potatoes cook, making a nice gravy.

22. Deep Fried Chitterlings

Chitterlings, popularly called chit'lings in the South, are the smaller intestines of swine. While not eaten as commonly today, they were very popular in times gone by. There are several ways to prepare chitterlings, but the deep fried variety is more agreeable than some other preparations.

Ingredients

Chitterlings
Salted water
1 tablespoon of whole cloves
1 red pepper, hot
1 egg, beaten
Cracker crumbs

Directions

Wash chitterlings thoroughly and cover with boiling salted water. Add 1 tablespoon of whole cloves and 1 red pepper cut in pieces. Cook until tender. Drain. Cut into pieces about the size of half dollars. Dip each piece in beaten egg and then in cracker crumbs. Deep fry until brown.

23. Souse Meat

Souse, or souse meat, is another example of the Southern passion to use every bit of their hogs. The tongue, ears, and feet are included in this recipe. Souse is normally served as a cold cut sandwich.

Ingredients

2 pork tongues
4 pig ears
2 pig feet
4 onions, chopped
2 tablespoons of salt
1 teaspoon of black pepper
15 black peppercorns, whole
3 tablespoons of dried sage
15 cloves, whole
2 tablespoons of pickling spice
½ teaspoon of garlic powder
3 cups of vinegar
2 pimentos, julienned
6 pepperoncini peppers, chopped
4 tablespoons of dill pickle relish
5 tablespoons of unflavored gelatin
1 cup of water

Directions

Place the pig tongues, pig ears, pig feet, and onions in a large pot. Add enough water to cover them. Season them with salt, black pepper, whole peppercorns, sage, cloves, pickling spice, garlic powder, and vinegar. Bring the mixture to a boil and cook for 2½ hours until the meat is done. Remove the meat from the pot. Strain the broth, and measure 8 cups of it into another pot. Simmer the broth. Peel the skin from ears, leaving them as intact as possible. Remove the gristle and fat from feet and combine them with the ear trimmings. Cut off a large portion of the tongue. Trim the loose meat from the remainder of the tongue and combine it with the other trimmings. Put the trimmings through a meat grinder, then stir them into the broth and let the mixture continue to simmer. Slice the tongue into thin strips and place them lengthwise into 2 glass loaf pans. Slice the ears into thin strips, then cut the strips into ½" pieces. Arrange the ear parts among the tongue strips. Divide the pimiento and the pepperoncini between the two molds. Sprinkle them with pickle relish. Dissolve the gelatin in 1 cup of water and stir it into the simmering broth. Ladle enough broth into each mold to completely cover the meat. Let it stand for 15 minutes, then cover it with remaining broth. Allow it to cool at room temperature for 2-3 hours until it begins to jell. Refrigerate for 8-10 hours.

II. Beef

Beef has always been an important part of Southern farming and ranching. While beef is more expensive to raise and feed than pork, the income opportunities as greater too.

There are many, many beef dishes from which to choose. Only 9 beef dishes are included here, but they are representative of the dishes Southerners prepared in past years. As is the case with other meat recipes in this volume, there are several variations possible, but the author has included the one he feels is most representative of the Southern tradition.

24. Hamburger-Bacon Roast

This great and easy to prepare dish combines 2 favorites – hamburger and bacon.

Ingredients

3 pounds of ground beef and pork
2 large potatoes, cooked and mashed
1 onion, chopped fine
2 slices of bread
Parsley, diced and chopped
Salt
Black pepper
3 hard cooked eggs
¼ pound of sliced bacon

Directions

Combine the meat, potatoes, onion, bread, and seasonings. Divide the mixture into 2 parts. Place one-half in a baking pan and cover it with the whole hard cooked eggs and the remaining half of mixture. Cover the meat with slices of bacon and bake it in a 400° oven for 1½ hours.

25, *Broiled Hamburger Steak*

This is another hamburger recipe. One pound of chopped beef will make 4 cakes. One can add mushroom sauce (see the recipe in Section IX) if desired.

Ingredients

1 pound of chopped beef
2 teaspoons of chopped onion
1 tablespoon of cold water
1 tablespoon of lard
Salt
Black pepper

Directions

Mix all ingredients together and shape them into small round cakes. Place a piece of butter on top of each cake and broil fast on both sides.

26. Veal Fricassee

Veal is the meat from a calf. A veal calf is raised until about 16 to 18 weeks of age, weighing up to 450 pounds. Male dairy calves are used in the veal industry. Dairy cows must give birth to continue producing milk, but male dairy calves are of little or no value to the dairy farmer. This recipe should be served with mushroom sauce.

Ingredients

2 pounds of veal loin
1 onion
2 stalks of celery
Carrot slices
Salt
Black pepper
Flour
Butter

Directions

Cut the 2 pounds of veal loin into portions. Cook them slowly in enough boiling water to cover them. Add 1 onion, 2 celery stalks, and 6 carrot slices. Remove the meat. Season it with salt and black pepper, then dredge the meat with flour and brown in butter.

27. Veal Steak

Ingredients

Veal steak, ½ inch thick
Salt
Black pepper
Flour
Lard
Paprika
2 onions, sliced
½ cup of sour cream

Directions

Cut the veal steak ½ inch thick. Season it with salt and black pepper and roll it in flour. Heat lard in a frying pan. Add the paprika until red, then add two sliced onions. Fry the vegetables slightly, then add the meat. Brown the meat all over, and gradually add ½ cup of sour cream. Cover the pan, let cook slowly for ½ hour, then add a little water and serve.

28. *Chipped Beef on Toast*

Chipped beef on toast ("SOS") is still served as a breakfast dish in the United States Army. It is not as common in the civilian world as it once was, but it is a tasty addition to eggs and hashbrowns.

Ingredients

½ pound of chipped smoked beef
½ cup of cream, sweet
1 cup of milk
1 tablespoon of butter
1 tablespoon of flour
Salt
Black pepper
Bread, toasted

Directions

Soak chipped beef in boiling water for 5 minutes. Drain and dry on a towel. Make a sauce by melting butter in top of double boiler, stir in the flour and blend the mixture well. Gradually add the milk and cream and cook for a few minutes. Add the seasonings and beef. Cook for 10 minutes and serve on crisp toast.

29. Boiled Beef Ribs

When we think of ribs, it is likely that baked or barbequed recipes come to mind. However, Southerners often boiled beef ribs. Here is once such recipe.

Ingredients

Beef short ribs
1 clove of garlic
1 onion, sliced
2 cups of tomato
Salt
Black pepper
1 teaspoon of paprika

Directions

Season the short ribs with salt and black pepper and rub a clove of garlic over them. Cover the ribs with boiling water, add 1 large, sliced onion. Cook the ribs slowly for 2 hours and then add 2 cups of tomatoes, one teaspoon of paprika, and cook the mixture slowly for another hour.

30. Beef Stew

There may be thousands of ways to make beef stew. The recipe below makes a lively lunch or dinner dish. This beef stew will caress the taste buds without overpowering them.

Ingredients

1½ of pounds lean beef
2 cups of tomatoes
1 large onion
1 green pepper, hot
1 cup of string beans
3 ears or 1 can of corn
2 carrots, sliced
Salt
Black pepper
Flour
Worcestershire sauce
Potatoes

Directions

Place 1½ pounds of lean beef into a deep skillet. Place as many potatoes as needed, tomatoes, onion, green pepper, string beans, corn, and carrots around the meat. Sprinkle the mixture well with salt and black pepper, and partially cover it with water. Cook the mixture slowly until the meat is done throughout. Add more water to the skillet if necessary to prevent the meat from drying out too much and becoming tough. Remove the mixture from the pan and it place on a serving platter and garnish with the vegetables. Add the necessary amount of flour to thicken the meat juices and make a savory gravy. Use chopped parsley and Worcestershire sauce for the final flavoring.

31. Corned Beef Hash

Corned beef hash is still a common dish served at any meal. Homemade corned beef hash is far, far superior to the canned variety found in stores.

Ingredients

2 tablespoons of butter
3 cups of boiled potatoes, cubed
¾ cup of sweet cream
3 teaspoons of parsley, finely chopped
2 cups of corned beef, precooked

Directions

Melt the butter in a double boiler. Add the potatoes and mix them in the butter. Then pour in the cream and add the corned beef and the chopped parsley. Stir the mixture well, but do not mash the potatoes. Place the mixture into a pan. Butter the top of the mixture and bake it until it is well browned. Garnish with a sprig of parsley.

32. Deep Fried Beef Liver

Beef liver is an excellent source of iron. The simple recipe presented here is a great dish for liver lovers.

Ingredients

1 pound of calves' liver, cut into 1" cubes
2 small onions, thinly sliced
2 sprigs of parsley
Lemon
Salt
Black pepper

Directions

Sprinkle the liver with salt and black pepper and cover it with the onions and parsley. Let it stand for 2 hours and then deep fry it at 390° for 1 minute. Drain, garnish with lemon and parsley

III. Chicken

By far, the top main ingredient in Southern main dishes is chicken. This is true for every area in the South. Southern farmers knew that chickens were easy to raise and keep and they didn't eat much. Just about the biggest worry farmers had with chickens was keeping foxes and weasels out of the henhouses.

Most farmers kept chickens for eggs. They ate some of the eggs and they sold the eggs they had left over.

Chicken is versatile and it can be prepared in hundreds of ways. This chapter only includes 22 of the many, many ways one can prepare chicken – Southern-style.

33. Country Fried Chicken

There is little more Southern than fried chicken. This recipe has an all-star lineup of Southern ingredients including chicken, cornmeal, and buttermilk.

Ingredients

1 small chicken
Salt a
Black pepper
Yellow cornmeal
Buttermilk
Egg yolks
Lard

Directions

Cut up the chicken into pieces and soak it for 2-3 hours in buttermilk, or even overnight in your refrigerator. Make sure there is enough buttermilk to come halfway up a breast piece. Too much buttermilk is better than too little. Melt the lard in a cast iron skillet (about ½" deep). Shake off the buttermilk and pat the chicken dry. Dip each piece of chicken in whisked egg yolks. Add salt and black pepper to the cornmeal in a brown paper bag. Add a few pieces of chicken to the bag and shake it well to cover. Remove the chicken from the bag and fry it a few pieces at a time at 350°-360° for about 24 minutes. Do not uncover the chicken. Turn the chicken frequently and carefully. The crust should be a golden light brown. Small pieces should be removed sooner if they are done. Remove the chicken pieces and add the salt.

34. Simple Fried Chicken

Here is another fried chicken recipe. This one is even easier to make than the previous one. This variety is great with fried chicken gravy (see the recipe in Section IX) or chicken sauce (see the recipe in Section IX).

Ingredients

1 chicken, young
Flour
Salt
Black pepper
1 tablespoon of lard

Directions

Select a young and tender fryer. Cut it into quarters. Dip the chicken into flour with salt and black pepper mixed into it. lard in an iron skillet and when hot, drop in pieces of chicken and brown quickly on all sides. Reduce the heat, add one cup of water, cover the skillet, and let the chicken simmer slowly until it is done. Remove the lid and let chicken fry down slowly.

35. Roast Chicken

Chicken is also delicious when roasted. The following recipe is terrific. One can use this recipe with turkey, but it will require more liquid and will have to be roasted longer if the turkey weighs more than 4 pounds.

Ingredients

1 seasoned chicken (4 pounds)
Flour
Butter
½ cup of chicken fat

Directions

Dredge a 4 pound seasoned chicken with flour and place it on its back in a dripping pan with chicken fat the size of an egg. Place the chicken in an oven preheated to 400°. When the flour is browned reduce the heat to 350°, then add ¼ cup of fat dissolved in ½ cup of boiling water and baste it every 15 minutes. Turn the chicken often until breast meat is tender which should about 1½ hours.

36. Broiled Chicken

Most any meat dish that can be baked can also be broiled. Chicken is no exception. This is an outstanding boiled chicken dish. Note: This recipe calls for precooking the chicken in butter sauce. Precooking the chicken in butter sauce assures the tenderness of the meat.

Ingredients

1 broiling chicken
1 pound of melted butter
4 parsley sprigs
1 small onion
¼ pound of mushrooms
1 garlic clove
Salt
Black pepper
Breadcrumbs

Directions

Clean the chicken and split it in half. Place it in a frying pan in which the butter has been melted. Chop the parsley, onion, mushrooms, and garlic and add to the mixture with salt and pepper. Cover the frying pan and allow the chicken to simmer for fifteen minutes, turning it occasionally so that the flavor is absorbed. Then dip the chicken in breadcrumbs and broil it until it is well browned. Flavor the chicken with the mushrooms, onion, garlic, and parsley mixture.

37. Barbecued Chicken

Barbecued chicken! Oh my, barbecued chicken! The very thought of this always magnificent and never disappointing dish activates the tastebuds and brings back great memories. This easy dish is intended to be grilled, but it can be made in an oven too. This recipe uses barbeque sauce (see the recipe in Section IX).

Ingredients

1 young broiling chicken
5 tablespoons melted butter
2 tablespoons vinegar
2 teaspoon dry mustard
½ teaspoon Worcestershire sauce
1 pinch red pepper

Directions

Split the chicken for broiling. Place it on a broiling rack, skin face down, and cook under moderate flame until well browned and almost tender. Turn and brown the other side. While chicken is cooking, baste frequently with barbecue sauce.

38. Chicken Pot Pie

Chicken pot pie continues to be a favorite dish in the Southland. It is easy and quick to make, and it can produce a lot of servings for the amount of chicken used. Thus, a poor family can stretch its food budget by serving chicken pot pie occasionally. This recipe uses homemade pie dough (see the recipe in Section IX).

Ingredients

1 young chicken
Pie dough
¼ cup of butter
Salt
Black pepper
1 cup of milk
¼ cup of chicken broth

Directions

Cut a 1½ pound chicken as if for frying. Place pieces into a stewpan and barely cover it with boiling water. Cook it slowly until the meat is tender.

Make pie dough but use a little less lard than called for in the recipe. Divide the dough into two parts.

Roll out one piece of dough very thinly. Line the sides of a baking dish with part of it, put in a layer of chicken, and dot it with butter, salt, and black pepper. Cut the rest of the piece of dough into strips, cover the chicken, alternating until all the chicken and dough are used. Add the milk and about ¼ cup of the stock in which the chicken was cooked. Roll out the second piece of dough, dot it with butter, fold it and roll it again until the butter is blended into the dough. Roll the dough out thinly, cover the top of the pie; press the edges together and make small slashes in the crust to allow the steam to escape. Bake the pie in an oven preheated to 400° until contents are cooked and the crust is well-browned. Chicken pot pie is usually served in the same dish in which it was baked.

39. Jambalaya

Jambalaya is a lively dish sure to make any meal more interesting. It is also an excellent way of utilizing leftovers. This recipe calls for leftover chicken, but veal or mutton can be substituted, if preferred.

Ingredients

1½ cups of cold chicken
1 cup of boiled rice
2 large celery stalks
½ green pepper
1 large onion, chopped
1½ cups of stewed tomatoes
Salt
Black pepper
Buttered breadcrumbs

Directions

Mix the chicken, rice, and tomatoes, and allow them to cook for ten minutes. Then add the chopped onion, green pepper, and celery. Turn the mixture into a baking dish and cover with buttered crumbs. Bake for 1 hour in an oven at 350°. Serve jambalaya while it is still very hot.

40. Chicken Stew

After a day of hunting or working on the farm, Southerners of old liked nothing better than sitting down to a hearty meal of chicken stew. In the past farm wives made stew in fireplaces or on stoves that burned wood. Today, women and men use modern appliances, but the result is the same – a delightful and filling entrée.

Ingredients

2 tablespoons of bacon grease
1 frying chicken (2-2½ pounds)
2 onions
3 cups of water
3 tomatoes, peeled and quartered
½ cup of cooking sherry
2 tablespoons of butter
½ cup of breadcrumbs
2 teaspoons of Worcestershire sauce
1 pound of fresh lima beans
Salt
Black pepper
½ cup of okra
3 ears of corn

Directions

Cut the chicken into small pieces and season it. Brown the onion in the bacon grease and then add the chicken to it. When the chicken is done, pour off the grease and put the chicken and onions in a Dutch oven. Add the water, tomatoes, sherry, and Worcestershire sauce.

Cook the mixture slowly over low heat for ½ hour, then add the lima beans, okra and corn cut from the cob. Let the stew simmer for 1 hour, then add the butter and breadcrumbs and cook ½ hour more.

41. Cream of Chicken Soup

This recipe doesn't contain chicken meat. But chicken broth is its main ingredient. It is great on a winter's day as either a main course or a side dish.

Ingredients

3 cups of chicken broth
3 tablespoons of rice
½ cup of diced celery
2 cups of hot milk
Parsley, chopped

Directions

Cook the rice and celery until they are soft. Strain them and add them to the chicken broth. Add 2 cups of hot milk, season the mixture with salt and pepper to taste. Sprinkle chopped parsley over the top just before serving.

42. Dixie Chicken Shortcake

This dish uses leftover chicken. It also includes Southern cornbread (see the recipe in Section IX). It doesn't get much more Southern than that.

Ingredients

1 large chicken, cooked
2 cups of chicken broth
2 tablespoons of flour
1 pound of mushrooms, cleaned
2 tablespoons of butter, melted
Salt
Black pepper
1 pan of Southern cornbread

Directions

Remove the skin and bones from the cooked chicken. Cut the meat into small pieces. Make a sauce, using 2 cups of the chicken broth and thickening it with the flour. Sauté the mushrooms in the butter. Add the chicken and mushrooms to the sauce. Cut the cornbread into 4 inch squares and split them. Cover the lower halves of the cornbread with some of the chicken mixture. Lay the cornbread crusts on top of the chicken mixture. Pour in the remaining chicken mixture.

43. Chicken Gumbo

Cumbo is rightfully identified with Louisiana, but it is a popular dish across the Southland. This particular variety of gumbo employs chicken as it star ingredient.

Ingredients

1 small stewing chicken
2 tablespoons of flour
3 tablespoons of butter, melted
1 onion, chopped
4 cups of okra, sliced and chopped
2 cups of tomato pulp
A few sprigs of parsley, chopped
4 cups of water
salt and pepper

Directions

Cut the chicken into serving portions. Dredge them lightly with the flour. Then sauté them in the butter, along with the chopped onion. When the chicken is nicely browned, add the okra, tomatoes, parsley, and water. Season the mixture to taste with salt and black pepper. Cook the mixture very slowly for about 2½ hours until the chicken is tender, and the okra is well cooked. Add water as required during the slow cooking process to create a thick soup. If you prefer a thinner soup, increase the quantity of water.

44. Chicken-Beef-Oyster Gumbo

As with almost all Southern dishes, there are many gumbo recipes. This one employs the triumvirate of chicken, beef, and oysters to create an empire of taste sensations.

Ingredients

1 small chicken
1 pound of beef cut for stewing
1 cup of diced okra
1 tablespoon of butter
1 onion
3 pints of water
24 oysters
Salt
Black pepper

Directions

Cut the chicken and stew it with the beef and 1 cup of okra in 3 pints of water. When a strong broth has been produced and the meat is tender, remove the chicken bones and cut the meat into small pieces. Add the oysters and their liquid and season the mixture to taste with salt, black pepper and onion browned in butter. Cook the mixture until the edges of the oysters curl.

45. Chicken Casserole

Chicken leftovers were always used in the South. The bones were fed to the family dogs and the meat was eaten by the humans. One great use for leftover chicken was cooking it in a casserole as in the following recipe.

Ingredients

2 cups of rice
2 cups of milk
1½ tablespoons of butter
2 eggs
1 cooked chicken
Salted water

Directions

Bone the chicken and cut it into 1" pieces. Boil the rice in salted water until the rice is tender. Stir in the butter, the milk, and the eggs. Put a layer of the mixture into a casserole dish. Then add the chicken. Bake the mixture at 350° until the chicken is well browned.

46. Chicken Hash

Another great use for leftover chicken is in a hash. Below is a recipe for great tasting and filling chicken hash.

Ingredients

2 tablespoons of butter
1½ tablespoons of flour
1 cup of chicken broth
2 cups of cooked chicken, chopped
Bread, toasted

Directions

Make a sauce with the flour and butter, using the chicken broth. When the sauce is thick, stir in the chicken. Place the mixture into a buttered casserole dish and bake. Garnish each helping with slices of toast.

47. Chicken Cakes

Chicken cakes are still another leftover chicken dish. To complete this dish, add celery to white sauce (see the recipe in Section IX) and the sauce pour over the cakes. Serve the chicken cakes on toast and garnish them with parsley.

Ingredients

1 cup of cooked chicken meat, chopped
2 eggs, slightly beaten
1 tablespoon of cream
Salt and pepper
Breadcrumbs, rolled fine
1 cup of white sauce
½ cup of finely chopped celery
Bread, toasted

Directions

Add 1 egg along with the cream, salt, and pepper to the chopped chicken. Fashion the mixture into small flat cakes. Dip the cakes in the other egg mixed with a little milk and roll the chicken in the breadcrumbs. Fry the chicken on both sides until well browned.

48. Chicken Chili

Southerners love their chili and chicken is a great replacement for beef in chili. In the There are several Southern chicken chili recipes. This one holds its own with any of them. Serve your chicken chili in a deep bowl with crackers or brown bread.

Ingredients

1 young chicken
2 tablespoons of salt
16 ounces of canned tomatoes
3 large onions, chopped
3 buttons of garlic, chopped
1½ teaspoons of chili powder
1 quart of chili beans, cooked
Water
Crackers or Brown bread

Directions

Cover the chicken with water and add the tomatoes, salt, 2 buttons of garlic, and 2 onions. Cook the chicken until it is done. Remove the chicken from the water and bone it and cut it into small pieces. Put the meat back into the liquid. Heat the water and while stirring it, add the chili powder. In a separate pan melt 2 tablespoons of butter and gently brown the remaining onion and garlic button in it. Add this to the original mixture and cook for 1 hour. When the mixture is nearly done, add 1 quart of cooked chili beans. Simmer for about another 10 minutes.

49. *Chicken and Dumplings*

Another dish closely related to the South is chicken and dumpling. In many chicken dishes farmers used young, tender chickens. Chicken and dumplings use older hens, because the cooking process will cause the meat to become tender.

Ingredients

1 chicken
1 cup of flour
2 teaspoons of baking powder
Milk
Salt and pepper
1 sprig of parsley
1 small onion, diced

Directions

Cut up the chicken, place it in a large pot and cover it with water. Add the chopped onion, salt, and pepper, and cook the chicken until it is tender. Mix the flour, baking powder, salt, minced parsley, and milk into a thick batter and drop it from the end of a spoon slowly into the pot. Cover the pot tightly and let the chickens and dumplings cook for 20 minutes without raising the lid.

Hint: If you use self-rising flour, the dumplings will be extra fluffy, and some people don't like that.

50. Chicken Stew

Chicken stew is always good, but it is especially welcome when it's cold outside. This great Southern dish is sure to warm you up even on the coldest days.

Ingredients

2 chickens
6 egg yolks, beaten
2 tablespoons of flour
¼ tablespoon of butter, melted
1 pint of milk
Salt and pepper
Crackers or brown bread

Directions

Boil two chickens until they are tender. Cut the meat from the bones and dice it. Beat the yolks of six eggs and set them aside. Blend two tablespoons of flour with ¼ pound of melted butter and add one pint of milk heated to the boiling point. Add the beaten yolks, season with salt and pepper to the milk and continue heating it. Add the diced chicken to the mix. Serve when all the ingredients are hot. Serve with crackers or brown bread.

51. Almond Chicken Soup

If one wants to go in a little different direction, he might want to try this Almond chicken soup. Almond chicken soup is a guaranteed nutty delight.

Ingredients

½ cup of blanched almonds
6 bitter almonds
3 cups of chicken broth
1 teaspoon of onion juice
3 tablespoons of butter
3 tablespoons of flour
2 cups of milk
1 cup of cream
Salt and pepper

Directions

Chop the almonds finely. The bitter almonds strengthen the flavor. Add the chopped almonds to the chicken broth, seasoned with the onion juice. Simmer the mixture slowly. Melt the butter and stir in the flour. When the butter and flour mixture is smooth, add it to the broth. Stir the chicken mixture constantly until it is boiling. Add the milk and cream and season to taste with salt and pepper.

52. *Baked Chicken Liver*

Baked chicken livers are healthy and hearty. They can be served as a main course, a snack, or as a side dish.

Ingredients

1 cup of raw chicken livers
1 tablespoon of butter
½ tablespoon of cream
2 tablespoons of milk
3 eggs
½ cup of mushrooms
Chopped parsley
Salt
Black pepper
Red pepper

Directions

Chop the liver, beat the yolks of eggs, and then add the cream and milk, butter, salt, pepper, parsley, and mushrooms. Place the liver and other ingredient mixture in buttered molds and cover the molds with greased paper. Put the molds in a pan of water and let them bake for 15-20 minutes.

53. Chicken-Ham Medley

Have leftover chicken and ham? What not mix them together for a super dish? Certainly, citizens of the old South thought that way. This little recipe makes a tremendous cold dish.

Ingredients

2 tablespoons of gelatin
¼ cup of cold water
4 cups of hot chicken broth
2 tablespoons of onion juice
1 cup chopped of cooked chicken
½ cup of chopped cooked ham
½ cup of chopped celery
1 pimiento, chopped fine

Directions

Soak the gelatin in cold water for 5 minutes. Add the hot chicken broth with the onion juice and stir until the gelatin dissolves. Set it aside to cool. When it begins to congeal, stir in the other ingredients, and it put in small molds. Chill. Serve on lettuce garnished with mayonnaise and parsley.

54. Southern Style Chicken Feet

The Southern penchant for avoiding waste can be found in another popular dish – chicken feet. Chicken feet is not only enjoyed in Asia, but it has also been eaten in the Southern United States for as long as there has been a South. This is a typical chicken feet recipe eaten across the Southland. One can enjoy chicken feet as a main course, a wholesome snack, or even as part of a larger meal. Chicken feet make a great alternative to hot wings.

Ingredients

1 pound of chicken feet
1 tablespoon of lard
1 onion, finely chopped
2 cloves of garlic, minced
1 bell pepper, diced
2 celery stalks, chopped
1 cup of chicken broth
1 teaspoon of paprika
½ teaspoon of cayenne pepper
Salt
Black pepper
Hot sauce

Directions

Melt the lard in a large pot on medium heat. Add the chopped onion, minced garlic, bell pepper, and celery. Sauté the mixture until the vegetables are soft and translucent. Add the chicken feet to the pot and stir well to coat them with the cooked vegetables. Pour in the chicken broth and season the mixture with paprika, cayenne pepper, salt, and black pepper. Stir everything together. Bring the mixture to a simmer, then reduce the heat to low. Cover the pot and let the mixture cook for about 2 hours, or until the chicken feet are tender and the flavors are well infused.

IV. Other Fowl

Chicken is the queen of Southern fowl dishes, but there are many other food birds, and many ways to prepare them. This chapter contains only 5 recipes, but many of the chicken recipes from the previous chapter can be applied to other kinds of fowl as well.

55. Roast Turkey

Roast turkey is popular around Thanksgiving time nowadays, but it was a common dish year round the Old South. This is a traditional recipe which means con can stuff the turkey with cornbread dressing (see the recipe in Section IX).

Ingredients

1 turkey of about 4 pounds, seasoned
Flour
Butter
¼ cup fat
½ cup of boiling water
Cornbread dressing

Directions

Dredge a four-pound a seasoned turkey with flour and place on its back in dripping pan with butter. Stuff the turkey with cornbread dressing. Place in an oven preheated to 400° and when the flour is browned reduce the heat to 350°. Then add ¼ cup of fat dissolved in ½ cup boiling water and baste every quarter of an hour. Turn the turkey often until breast meat is tender, then it is done. About 1½ hours are required for the process. Larger turkeys will require more liquid and will have to be roasted longer according to size.

56. Roast Duck

Roast duck is a tasty Southern dish that remains popular. This recipe calls for the use of bread stuffing (see the recipe in Section IX), apple stuffing (see the recipe in Section IX) or chestnut stuffing (see the recipe in Section IX). It also uses Guava jelly (see the recipe in Section IX).

Ingredients

1 duck
Salt
Black pepper
2 tablespoons of ginger, ground
1 onion
4 cloves
Stuffing, bread, apple, or chestnut
Guava jelly
Water

Directions

Rub the duck with salt and black pepper. Take 2 tablespoons of ground ginger and rub on both the inside and outside of the duck. Peel one onion, stick 4 cloves into it and place it on the duck. Place the duck in a roaster and add 1 cup of water. Roast the duck and bast it often. Add water when necessary. Stuff the duck with bread, apple, or chestnut stuffing. The gravy should be highly seasoned and guava jelly may be added last.

57. *Roast Partridge and Bacon*

The Southern people also enjoyed a well roasted duck and bacon dish with a garnish of baked oranges (see the recipe in Section IX).

Ingredients

4 partridges
4 strips of bacon
Salt
Black pepper
1 cup of sour cream
Bread, toasted
Baked oranges
1 cup of water

Directions

Pin over the breast of the partridges a long thin strip of bacon. Rub the outside and inside of the partridges with salt and black pepper. Put the partridges in a roasting pan with 1 cup of water. Roast the ducks in a hot oven for 30 minutes, basting every 5 minutes. When the birds and the gravy are rich brown, pour a cup of sour cream over them. Let the cream bubble up in the pan for 1 minute, baste the partridges once more, and serve them on toast with the gravy poured over them. Garnish the partridges with baked oranges.

58. Pigeon Pie

Pigeon is usually considered an Asian dish, but it was very popular in the South as well. This nice pot pie includes homemade dough (see the recipe in Section IX.

Ingredients

4 squabs, parboiled
Pie dough
3 tablespoons butter, melted
3 tablespoons flour
2 cups broth in which squabs were boiled
1 cup milk
Salt
Black pepper
Buttered breadcrumbs

Directions

Fry the parboiled squabs until they are browned. Line a deep casserole pan with pie dough and place the fried squabs in it. Blend 3 tablespoons of flour with the melted butter and stir it slowly into the pigeon stock and milk. Season the stock with salt and black pepper and heat it until it is thickened. Pour the sauce over the squabs. Sprinkle buttered breadcrumbs on top of the pie and place it in an oven preheated to 450° and cook it for 10 minutes. Reduce the heat to 350°-375° and continue baking for 8-10 minutes, until the crumbs and the edges of crust are nicely browned.

59. Squab Stuffed with Bacon

Southerners, it seems, thought bacon took every meat dish to a new level. The author still does. But whether that is true or not in most cases, it is true of this dish, The squab would taste great without the bacon, but stuffed with it, it is special.

Ingredients

4 squabs
6 slices of bacon
1 onion
¾ cup of chopped celery
2 cups of rice
4 cups of chicken broth
4 eggs
Salt
Black pepper
Mustard
Pickle juice

Directions

Fry the diced bacon until it is crisp. Remove the bacon and brown the chopped celery and onions in the bacon drippings. Boil the rice in the chicken stock until tender, then add the bacon, celery, and onion. Beat the eggs and add them to the rice. Season with salt and pepper. Stuff the squabs with the mixture and make mounds of the remaining filling on which to lay the squab. Bake the squabs in a hot oven for about 25 minutes, basting them frequently with the mustard and pickle juice.

V. Fish and Seafood

When we think of the South most of us don't automatically think of seafood. Yet, there are thousands of miles of coastline from Virginia to Florida and on to Texas. Beyond that, there are thousands of miles of rivers and streams inland. With that much water teeming with fish and other aquatic animals, it is no wonder that the South has produced thousands upon thousands of seafood dishes.

This section looks at just 30 of the many, many great Southern fish and seafood dishes. They are certain to please.

60. *Southern Deep Fried Catfish*

What dish is more closely identified with the Suth than catfish? Because of the close connection, it is only natural that a fried catfish dish lead off this section. This catfish dish is served with another of the South's favorite side dishes – hushpuppies. In fact, it is difficult to think of catfish without thinking of hot and crunchy hushpuppies (see the recipe in Section IX).

Ingredients

½ cup of buttermilk
½ cup of water
Salt
Black pepper
1 pound of catfish fillets, cut into strips
1½ cups of cornmeal, fine
½ cup of flour
Lard

Directions

Mix the buttermilk, water, salt, and black pepper in a small bowl. Pour the mixture into a flat pan large enough to hold the fillets. Arrange the fillets in a single layer in the pan, turning them to coat each side. Set them aside to marinate. Combine the cornmeal, flour, and seafood seasoning in a 2 gallon plastic bag. Add the fillets to the bag, a few at a time, and tumble gently until they are evenly coated. Heat the lard in a deep fryer to 365°. Fry the fillets in hot the hot lard for 3 minutes until they are crisp and golden brown. Work in batches to avoid overcrowding. This will leave the fillets room to brown properly.

61. Lobster made with Madeira

In savory dishes, Madeira wine complements the flavor of meats and fish. This lobster dish curdles quickly and should be made just in time to serve immediately.

Ingredients

2 cups of boiled lobster meat
2 tablespoons of butter
1 cup of Madeira wine
1 cup of cream
2 egg yolks
¼ teaspoon of salt
Cayenne pepper

Directions

Melt the butter in a saucepan and add the lobster, which has been previously cut into small pieces. Cover the pan and let the lobster simmer slowly for 5 minutes, then add the wine and cook the lobster for 3 minutes. Beat the egg yolks and to them add the cream. Mix the eggs and cream and add the mixture to the lobster. Shake the pan until the mixture is thickened. If the mixture is stirred it will break up the lobster.

62. *Lobster made with Sauterne*

Sauterne is a salted white cooking wine, with a distinct sweet flavor. It is part of many recipes including this one featuring lobster.

Ingredients

4 cups of lobster meat, broken in small pieces
1 pound of fresh mushrooms
1 cup of Sauterne wine
1 pint of rich cream
2 egg yolks
1 tablespoon of flour
2 tablespoons of butter
Breadcrumbs
Parmesan cheese
Paprika

Directions

Sauté the mushrooms in the butter. Cover them tightly while cooking. Season the mushrooms with the wine and add the rich cream to which the beaten egg yolks have been added. Thicken with the flour. When smooth, add the lobster. Place in a buttered lobster shell which has been cut lengthwise. Dot the lobster with butter, then sprinkle it with paprika and breadcrumbs mixed with the parmesan cheese. Place the lobster in an oven and bake until it is a delicate brown.

63. Crayfish Soup

Crayfish, often called "crawdads," are the freshwater version of lobster. However, they don't usually get as large as their ocean cousins. While this recipe may seem complicated, it is easy to make.

Ingredients

24 crayfish
1 quart of water
2 onions
2 carrots
2 stalks of celery
4 branches of parsley
¼ teaspoon of thyme
6 tablespoons of cracker crumbs
Milk
3 tablespoons of butter
2 tablespoons of flour
Salt
Black pepper
1 egg, beaten

Directions

Prepare the crayfish for soup by soaking it in cold water for 30 minutes. When it is cleaned, place the crayfish in a soup pot with the water, 1 onion, the carrots, the celery, half the quantity of parsley and the thyme. Allow the water to come to a boil and cook the crayfish for 25 minutes. Drain off the water from the crayfish and set it aside for later use. Remove all the meat from the heads and bodies of the crayfish. Set aside the heads which are to be stuffed. Moisten the cracker crumbs with milk. Chop the crayfish meat and add it to the moistened crumbs. Mince the remaining onion, melt the butter, and add the onion and 1 tablespoon of flour. Add 1 tablespoon of the fish broth and the remainder of the parsley. Season it with salt and pepper to taste. Simmer the mixture slowly for a few minutes. Add the crayfish and bread crumb mixture and cook it for 2 minutes longer. Remove it from the stove and let cool slightly. Stir in the beaten egg and fill the crayfish heads with the mixture. Dredge the heads in flour and fry them in butter until they are nicely browned. Drain them on paper and keep them warm while preparing the stock. Melt the balance of the butter, add the remainder of the flour, and stir until smooth. Strain the reserved stock to remove the celery and carrots. Add the broth to the butter and flour. Cook the mixture slowly for 12 minutes. Season it with more salt and pepper if desired. Before serving, add the stuffed crayfish heads.

64. Pickled Shrimp Paste

Shrimp paste makes for an excellent appetizer or side dish. It is easy to prepare and will add a little class to any affair.

Ingredients

1 quart of pickled shrimp
Salt
Black pepper
Ginger, ground
2 teaspoons of butter

Directions

Run a quart of picked shrimp through a meat grinder. After grinding it, put the shrimp into a saucepan with salt, pepper, ginger and two heaping tablespoons of butter. Heat it thoroughly, and place it into molds, pressing it down very hard with a spoon while pouring the melted butter over top. Refrigerate it. When it is cold, slice and serve it.

65. *Shrimp Gumbo*

There is, it seems, a gumbo recipe for most kinds of meat. This gumbo features shrimp.

Ingredients

2 quarts of fresh shrimp
3 onions
½ cup of vinegar
2 quarts water
1 tablespoon of butter, melted
1 tablespoon of flour
4 cups of okra, cut fine
1 cup of cooked rice
6 large tomatoes, skinned
Salt
Sugar
Black pepper

Directions

Clean the shrimp and boil them with 2 onions, vinegar, and salt in the water for about 20 minutes. Drain off the stock and save it. Shell the shrimp. Chop the remaining onion and brown it in the melted butter. Mix in the flour and slowly add the strained broth, stirring it constantly. Add the okra, rice, tomatoes, seasonings, and the shelled shrimp. Let the mixture simmer for a short time to cook the okra and tomatoes before serving the dish.

66. Shrimp Salad with Green Peas

A nice cold salad is always welcome. The stars of this salad are shrimp and green peas.

Ingredients

1 cupful of fresh shrimp
½ cup of diced celery
2 hard cooked eggs
½ cup of green peas

Directions

This works well as a cold plate. with one tablespoon each of celery, chopped eggs and peas placed around the tablespoon of shrimp, in which case you would need almost a whole cup of celery. Or you may mix all the ingredients lightly together with mayonnaise, first thinning the mayonnaise with cream and seasoning, and serve as a salad on crisp lettuce.

67. Deep Fried Shrimp and Rice

Shrimp and rice work well together and make a really good dish.

Ingredients

1 cup of rice
2 eggs
1 tablespoon of butter
2 quarts of shrimp, finely minced
Salt
Black pepper
Breadcrumbs
Lard

Directions

After cooking the rice, add the butter while the rice is still hot. Beat the eggs slightly and add the finely minced shrimp. Season with the salt and black pepper to taste then roll the mixture in shapes. Then dip the shrimp in breadcrumbs and the eggs. Fry in lard.

68. Shrimp Cocktail

Even many of those that don't care for shrimp enjoy a zesty shrimp cocktail. This recipe meets the definition of zesty.

Ingredients

Boiled shrimp
Avocado
2 tablespoons of mayonnaise
2 tablespoons of ketchup
1 tablespoon of fresh tomato, finely chopped
1 tablespoon of green peppers, finely chopped
Chili sauce

Directions

Take an equal portion of boiled shrimp and fresh avocado, cut into small pieces, and serve them with a sauce made by stirring together 2 tablespoons of mayonnaise, 2 tablespoons ketchup, 1 tablespoon each of finely chopped fresh tomatoes, finely chopped green peppers, and chili sauce.

69. Haddock and Shrimp Stew

Haddock may not be the first among food fish lovers. But accompanied by shrimp, haddock makes a fine stew.

Ingredients

1 tablespoon of salt
1 pound of fresh shrimp
12 cloves
½ pound of fresh mushrooms
2 tablespoons of butter
2 large onions, chopped
2 buds of garlic
2 cups of tomato pulp
2 cups of water
1½ teaspoons of curry powder
1 cup of grated cheese
½ cup of sherry
2 pounds of haddock fillets
1 pound of scallops
2 tablespoons of flour
Bread, toasted

Directions

Add the shrimp, 4 cloves and salt to 1½ quarts of water and bring them to a boil. After boiling them for 10 minutes remove the shrimp from the pot, saving the broth for later use. Shell the shrimp and cut them in half lengthwise. Cut the mushrooms into thin slices, add to the shrimp. and allow them to stand until needed. Melt the butter and fry the onions and garlic in it until golden brown. Add the tomato pulp and 2 cups of water, 4 cloves, curry powder, cheese and ¼ cup of sherry. Allow this mixture to cook slowly for 30 minutes. Season with more salt, if desired. Meanwhile, bring shrimp broth to boiling point, add the fillets of fish, scallops, 4 cloves and ½ cup of sherry. Lower the flame and simmer for about 15 minutes until the fish is sufficiently cooked. Combine the shrimp and mushroom mixture with the fish and cook for 5 minutes. Moisten the flour with a little cold water and add it to the boiling liquid as a slight thickening. Cook for another 5 minutes. Remove pieces of fish from the sauce and place them on buttered slices of toast on a large platter. Pour the sauce over fish and serve.

70. Boiled Shrimp

Boiled shrimp is very easy to prepare and is perfect for those that enjoy shrimp's special favor. Canned shrimp can be used in this recipe, if desired.

Ingredients

1 pound of fresh shrimp
2 large ripe tomatoes
1 celery stalk
¼ teaspoon of paprika
½ teaspoon of salt
Mayonnaise

Directions

Drop shrimp into boiling salt water and cook it for 15 minutes. When the shrimp is cool, remove the shells and set it aside to chill. Peel the tomatoes and chop them fine. Add finely chopped celery and combine the mixture with the shrimp and tomatoes. Season liberally with paprika and salt and add sufficient mayonnaise to moisten. Mix the ingredients well and serve the dish cold.

71. Shrimp Stuffed Pompano

Fresh pompano can be hard to find. Other fish such as snapper, mahi-mahi, grouper, seabass, and amberjack may be used instead of pompano in the recipe below. This recipe makes use of homemade French dressing (see the recipe in Section IX).

Ingredients

2 cups of cooked shrimp
2 eggs
1 cup of rich cream
1 boned pompano
½ cup of chopped mushrooms
¼ cup of sherry
Black pepper
Salt
Paprika
Cucumbers
French dressing

Directions

Clean the shrimp and put them through a meat grinder. Beat the eggs and half of the cream together. Mix the shrimp, mushrooms and seasoning together and stir in the cream and eggs. Stir until it is a smooth paste. Put the mixture on one half of the pompano. Sew the two halves of the fish together and put it in a baking dish. Pour the remaining cream over the fish and bake at a moderate heat for 45 minutes.

Serve garnished with sliced cucumbers which have been marinated in French dressing.

72. Browned Oysters

Browned oysters are often used as a side dish, but they can make for a nice entrée as well.

Ingredients

1 quart of oysters
4 tablespoons of butter
1½ tablespoons of flour
Juice of one lemon
Salt
Black pepper
Worcestershire sauce

Directions

Remove the oysters from their juice and drain. Dredge them in flour and fry them in two tablespoons of butter until they are brown. Remove the oysters from the pan and strain the juice through a colander or a sieve. Make a brown sauce of the remaining butter and flour by adding the juice from the cooked oysters. Add the lemon juice and a dash of Worcestershire sauce, pour over the oysters, and serve.

73. Fried Oysters

This simple fried oyster recipe makes for a nice dish any seafood lover will enjoy.

Ingredients

1 quart of oysters
2 eggs
Lard
Cracker crumbs

Directions

Wash and drain the oysters. Beat the eggs. Dip the oysters into the cracker crumbs, then into the egg, and then back into the crumbs. Have the lard hot and fry the oysters quickly. Drain on brown paper.

74. Oyster Loaf

Oyster loaf is one of those pleasing dishes that is often served on special occasions. It uses French bread (see the recipe in Section IX).

Ingredients

1 loaf of French bread
24 oysters
½ cup of cream
1 tablespoon of chopped celery
Salt
Black pepper
2 drops of tabasco sauce

Directions

Cut off the top the crust of a loaf of French bread and scoop out the inside. Butter ½ of the scooped out portion and toast it in an oven. Fry 2 dozen oysters in butter, add ½ cup of cream, a tablespoon of chopped celery, black pepper, salt, two drops of tabasco sauce, and toasted bread. Fill the hollowed loaf with the mixture and cover it with the top crust and bake it for 20 minutes, basting it frequently with the juice from the oysters. Slice the loaf and serve it hot.

75. Oyster Casserole

Casseroles were common dishes prepared in Southern kitchens and this book contains several of them. This casserole recipe features oysters.

Ingredients

12 oysters
3 tablespoons of butter
2 tablespoons of red pepper, chopped
2 teaspoons of chopped onions
3 tablespoons of flour
Cayenne pepper, a few grains
½ cup of parmesan cheese
Salt
Black pepper

Directions

Parboil the oysters, then remove them from the pan. Add enough water to the fluid to make 1½ cups. Melt the butter and fry the onion and red pepper in it. Add the flour to the onion and pepper, and blend. Gradually pour on the juice and stir the mixture constantly. Bring the mixture to a boil and season it. Arrange the oysters in a casserole dish. Pour the liquid over them, add the grated cheese and a few grains of cayenne pepper, and bake them in the oven until they are thoroughly heated.

76. Oyster Pie

Oyster pie is a nice dish that is easy to make. This recipe employs white sauce (see the recipe in Section IX).

Ingredients

2 cups of white sauce
Celery salt
1 teaspoon of onion juice
12 oysters
1 pie crust

Directions

Mix the celery salt, onion juice and the oysters into the white sauce. Season the mixture to taste and cover it with a pie crust. Bake the pie for 20 minutes in a preheated 450° oven, or until the pie crust is done.

77. Creamy Oyster Stew

Oyster stew is a high profile dish that was served when Southerners felt like something simple that seemed really special.

Ingredients

1 quart of oysters
1 quart of milk
1 tablespoon of flour
1 tablespoon of butter
½ cup of chopped celery
1 green pepper
Worcestershire sauce
Salt
Black pepper

Directions

Put the oysters through a meat grinder. Make a cream soup with milk, thickened with flour, and seasoned with the butter, salt, black pepper, chopped celery, and green pepper. Add the oysters and keep the soup hot but do not allow it to boil or it might curdle. Add a little Worcestershire sauce just before serving.

78. Strained Oyster Soup

Here is another dish for oyster lovers. It makes a great prelude to the main course.

Ingredients

1 quart of oysters
1 quart of rich milk
2 tablespoons of butter
1 tablespoon of parsley, finely chopped
1 teaspoon of onion juice
Salt
Black pepper

Directions

Strain the oysters and put the oyster broth in a saucepan. Pour the milk into a double boiler. Heat the oyster broth but do not let it come to a boil. When both are hot, add the broth to the milk and stir. Add the butter and the seasoning, then gradually put the oysters in one by one and heat until it is hot, but never let it boil. When the oysters puff and the edges crinkle, serve them at once.

79. Crab Soup

Lively carb soup is a terrific addition to any spicy meal. This recipe includes scalded milk. Scalded milk is milk that is heated to a temperature of about 180° and then cooled down to about 110°.

Ingredients

2 tablespoons of butter
1 onion, finely chopped
1 tablespoon of flour
2 cups of warm water
1 cup of crab meat
¾ cup of chopped celery
Parsley, chopped
Salt
Black pepper
Tabasco sauce
3 cups of scalded milk

Directions

Melt the butter. Brown the onion in it. Blend in the flour and add the warm water slowly. Allow the mixture to cook until it is slightly thickened. Add the crab meat, celery, parsley, and seasonings. Allow the mixture to simmer for 30 minutes. Just before serving, add the scalded milk.

80. Deep Fried Crab

Southerners have always loved their deep fried foods. This recipe for deep fried crabs is a good example of this. This recipe utilizes white sauce (see the recipe in Section IX).

Ingredients

2 cups of crab meat, finely chopped
1 teaspoon of onion juice
Salt and pepper
Parsley, chopped
1 cup of white sauce
Cracker crumbs
1 egg, beaten

Directions

Chop the crab meat finely and add the seasonings. Mold the mixture into croquettes, roll them in cracker crumbs, and dip them in the slightly beaten egg. Then roll them in the crumbs again. Deep fry them in lard until they are golden brown. Then add them to the white sauce.

81. Deviled Crabs

Ingredients

1 pint of crab meat
1 tablespoon of butter
1 tablespoon of flower
½ cup of cream
2 hardboiled eggs, chopped
Salt
Black pepper
1 parsley sprig
Worcestershire sauce
Cracker crumbs

Directions

Make a white sauce by mixing one tablespoonful of melted butter and one tablespoonful of flour. Add ½ cup of cream and let it come to a boil, stirring it constantly. Add salt and pepper. Then add one pint of crab meat, two chopped hardboiled eggs, a sprig of parsley, and a dash of Worcestershire sauce. Split the mixture into several equal parts and place them in a muffin pan. Brush them with melted butter and cracker crumbs and bake them slowly until they are well browned.

82. *Creamy Crab Soup*

Crab soup can be served either as a main course, or as a prelude to a larger, heavier meal. Leftovers can be refrigerated and served for the next day's lunch.

Ingredients

1 tablespoon of flour
2 tablespoons of butter
2 quarts of milk
1 pint of crab meat
½ onion sliced
½ pint of whipped cream
Parsley. chopped
Celery
Salt
Black pepper

Directions

Melt the butter in the top of a double boiler, add the flour and blend it. Gradually add the milk and onion, parsley and celery and season the mixture to taste. Cook the mixture slowly until the soup thickens a little, then add the crab meat. Serve in individual dishes with a spoonful of whipped cream on top.

83. Codfish Cakes

Codfish cakes can be whipped up quickly and served alone for lunch or dinner. They can also be served with a nice tomato sauce (see the recipe in Section IX).

Ingredients

2 cups of cold boiled codfish, flaked
2 cups of mashed potatoes
1 tablespoon of butter
1 egg, beaten
Salt
Black pepper

Directions

Mix all the ingredients together. Shape the mixture into round flat cakes and dredge in flour. Then fry them on both sides in butter.

84. Baked Herring

Baked herring is a another one of those dishes that we may not immediately associate with the South the way we do catfish. But this dish is certainly Southern in every respect.

Ingredients

1 herring
Flour
Butter
Parsley
1 Lemon, sliced

Directions

Cover the herring with cold water and soak it overnight. Drain the water off, roll the fish lightly in flour and place it in a baking pan. Dot it with butter and cook it in an oven preheated to 400° until it is tender. Place the fish on a hot platter and serve it with a little melted butter poured over the fish. Garnish it with parsley and sliced lemon.

85. Broiled Mackerel

Broiled Atlantic Mackerel is an old-time dish served in the South dish. This this recipe calls for fresh mackerel, not the canned variety.

Ingredients

Mackerel
Salt
Black Pepper
Cayenne Pepper
Butter
Lemon Juice

Directions

Wash the mackerel and split it in half. Season the fish with black pepper and salt and place it on a well-greased broiler pan and put it in an oven preheated to 550°. Broil the fish on both sides until it is tender. Place the mackerel on a hot platter and sprinkle it with cayenne pepper. Serve the fish with a sauce made of three tablespoons of melted butter and lemon juice.

86. Fried Flounder Fillets

The next recipe features flounder fillets covered with tomato sauce (see the recipe in Section IX).

Ingredients

5 flounder fillets
3 tablespoons of butter
1 cup of milk
Breadcrumbs (sifted)
1 egg
1 cup of tomato sauce
Salt
Black pepper

Directions

Combine the egg, milk, salt, and black pepper. Soak the fish in this mixture for 15 minutes. Dip each fillet in the breadcrumbs. Allow frying pan with butter to become hot before placing fillets in it. Fry the fish on both sides until it is browned, then pour tomato sauce over all of it.

87. Deep Fried Frog Legs

Southern ponds and streams have always teemed with frogs and Southerners have always harvested them. Deep fried frog legs can make a main course, but they are more often served as a side dish or an appetizer. This recipe calls for serving two frog legs per person.

Ingredients

8 frog legs
½ cup of lemon juice
Salt
Black pepper
1 egg, beaten
Cracker crumbs
Salt water

Directions

Only the hind legs of the frogs are eaten. Skin the legs and scald them in boiling salt water and lemon juice for about two minutes. Dry the legs after scalding them. Season the legs with salt and black pepper. Dip the legs in beaten egg and then in cracker crumbs. Fry the frog legs for 3 minutes in lard.

88. Turtle and Veal Bone Soup

Turtles have always been common in Southern inland waterways. This recipe combines veal bones (another example of the Southern penchant for using everything possible) and turtle in a surprisingly hearty dark meat dish. Although there are a lot of ingredients, the dish is simple to make.

2 pounds of veal bones
2 carrots
2 onions
2 tablespoons of butter
3 tablespoons of flour
2 quarts of beef stock
1 small can of tomatoes
1 small can of tomato puree
Salt
Black pepper
Whole cloves
½ cup sherry
2 cups of fresh turtle meat, boiled
1 lemon
2 hardboiled eggs, chopped

Directions

Roast the veal bones and vegetables with the butter until they are brown. Add the flour and brown the mixture again. Add the beef stock, tomatoes, tomato puree, salt, black pepper, and a few whole cloves. Boil the mixture for 2 hours. Add the sherry. Strain the soup. Cut the boiled turtle meat into small squares and add it, the lemon, and the chopped eggs. Boil everything quickly and serve the soup while piping hot.

89. Baked Shad

Nowadays, Southerners are more likely to use shad as fishing bait than as food, but there are shad recipes from years ago that are still around today. This is one of them.

Ingredients

1 shad, 3-4 pounds
½ cup of melted butter
Salt
Black pepper
Mashed potatoes
Parsley
Lemon slices

Directions

Clean and bone the fish. Broil it for 10 minutes and then place it on a buttered plank, skin side down. Season the fish well and pour melted butter over it. Bake for 15 minutes in an oven preheated to 400°. Remove the fish from the oven and place mounds of mashed potatoes around it. Place the fish and potatoes into the oven and cook them until the potatoes are brown and fish is well done. Garnish the dish with parsley and lemon slices.

VI. Sheep and Goat

Fewer Southern farmers of the past kept sheep and goats than kept swine and cattle. However, many did, and the animals were important sources of revenue. They were also sources of food. This section relates 5 representative sheep and goat recipes, but there were many others.

90. Roast Leg of Lamb

Leg of lamb is perhaps the most popular lamb dish. Many lamb dishes are served with one sort of mint jelly or another. This one is served with mint ice (see the recipe in Section IX).

Ingredients

5 pounds of leg of lamb
4 cloves of garlic, sliced
Salt
Black pepper
2 tablespoons of fresh rosemary

Directions

Preheat an oven to 350°. Cut deep slits on the top of leg of lamb every 3-4 inches. Push slices of garlic down into the slits. Season the lamb generously with salt and black pepper. Place the lamb on a roasting pan and arrange several sprigs of fresh rosemary under and on top of it. Roast the lamb in the preheated oven for up to 2 hours until it is medium rare to medium done. Cover the lamb and it let rest for at least 10 minutes before carving it.

91. Barbecued Lamb

Barbecued lamb is another dish common to the South. This recipe includes homemade chili sauce (see the recipe in Section IX).

Ingredients

1 leg of lamb
2 tablespoons of chili sauce
2 onions (sliced)
1 clove of garlic
1 tablespoon of Worcestershire sauce
1 teaspoon of ginger, ground
1 teaspoon of dry mustard
1 tablespoon of vinegar
Flour
Black pepper
Salt
1 cup of water, boiling
2 tablespoons of olive oil

Directions

Mix all the spices together and after wiping the lamb well with a damp cloth, rub it thoroughly with the spice mixture. Dredge the lamb well with flour and brown it for about 25 minutes in an oven preheated to 400°. Reduce the heat and baste the lamb with a sauce made by mixing the chili sauce, Worcestershire sauce, vinegar, and olive oil together. Slice the onion and place it around the meat with the clove of garlic. Baste the lamb every 15 minutes, allowing about 30 minutes to the pound for roasting. 1 hour before the cooking is finished, add 1 cup of boiling water. Skim the fat from the pan and strain for gravy.

92. *Sweetbreads and Chicken*

Sweetbread is the common name for the thymus or pancreas of a calf or lamb. Sweetbreads have a rich, slightly gamey flavor and a tender, succulent texture. This and the next recipe employ lamb sweetbreads. This recipe teams chicken and sweetbreads in an enticing dish.

Ingredients

2 pairs of lamb sweetbreads
1 large chicken, cooked
1 quart of cream
1 tablespoon of cornstarch
Milk
2 egg yolks
1 tablespoon of butter
Salt
Red pepper
Bread, toasted
1 glass of sherry

Directions

Parboil the sweetbreads, and then let them cool. Remove all the membrane and cut the sweetbreads into small pieces. Cut cooked chicken and add it to the sweetbreads. Place the cream in a double boiler and thicken it with the cornstarch which has been dissolved in a little milk. When the cream has been heated thoroughly, add the egg yolks, and stir the mixture well. Add the butter and the seasoning. When the mixture is well thickened and hot, stir in the chicken and sweetbreads. Just before serving add one glass of sherry. Serve on toast.

93. Sweetbreads Casserole

This terrific and typically Southern casserole dish is accented with mushrooms.

Ingredients

1 pair lamb of sweetbreads
2 tablespoons of butter, melted
2 tablespoons of flour
Salt
Black pepper
2 cups of milk
Breadcrumbs
1 pound of fresh mushrooms

Directions

Parboil the sweetbreads and remove all the loose membranes. Sauté the sweetbreads in 1 tablespoon of butter. Blend in 1 tablespoon of the flour. Add salt and black pepper to taste and 1 cup of the milk. Simmer them slowly until they are thickened. Wash and peel the mushrooms, then sauté them in the remaining butter. Blend in the remaining flour and add the salt and black pepper and milk. When the mushroom mixture is thickened, combine it with the sweetbread mixture and put it all in a casserole dish. Cover the sweetbread with breadcrumbs and dot it with butter. Brown the mixture in an oven preheated to 400° for 5-8 minutes.

94. Goat Stew

Goat is not as popular a dish in the South as it was in decades past, but it is still prepared in several different ways. Here is a nice stew that features goat as its signature ingredient. It also includes tomato sauce (see the recipe in Section IX).

Ingredients

1 pound of goat meat, cut into large chunks
¼ cup of vinegar
4 cloves of garlic, crushed
1 tablespoon of lard
1 onion, chopped
1 bell pepper, cut into 1 inch squares
1 cup of tomato sauce
2 cups of beef stock
1 potato, peeled and cut into large chunks
2 carrots, peeled and cut into large chunks
½ cup of green peas
½ teaspoon of salt
¼ teaspoon of black pepper
Cayenne pepper

Directions

Mix the goat meat with the vinegar and garlic in a large bowl. Cover and refrigerate the goat meat and let it marinate for 6 hours. Remove the meat from the marinade and pat it dry. Save the marinade and garlic separately. Heat the lard in a large pot over medium heat. Working in batches, cook goat meat in shortening for 10-15 minutes, stirring it occasionally, until it is browned. Transfer the goat meat to a plate and set it aside. Save the drippings in the pot. Add the onion, bell pepper, and saved garlic to the drippings. Cook and stir the mixture over medium heat for about 5 minutes until onion is caramelized. Pour in the tomato sauce and bring the mixture to a simmer. Cook the sauce for about 5 minutes until it is slightly thickened. Return the goat meat to sauce. Pour in the beef stock and saved marinade and bring the mixture to a boil. Reduce the heat to low, cover the pot, and let it simmer for 30-40 minutes until meat is partially tender. Stir in the potato, carrots, and peas and season with the salt, black pepper, and cayenne pepper. Simmer the mixture for another 20-30 minutes until goat meat is very tender and potato and carrots are cooked through.

VII. Wild Game

In the days of yore most rural Southerners supplemented their diets by hunting wild game. In those days there was an ample amount of wild meat to fill any holes in a farm family's food supply. Wild game recipes matched the wild game in abundance. This section only presents 5 of the hundreds of wild game dishes that graced Southern tables in the past.

95. *Roast Rabbit*

Rabbit reproduced prolifically and there were always hundreds of the furry little critters to be had. Southerners hunted rabbits, often with dogs, and usually in the fall and winter. Every farm family looked forward to a "mess" of fresh rabbit on the table. This roast rabbit recipe was common in those days.

Ingredients

1 rabbit, cut in portions
1 cup of flour
2 eggs, beaten
4 tablespoons of butter, melted
1 small onion, minced
Salt
Black pepper
Water, hot
Cracker crumbs

Directions

Wash the pieces of rabbit and wipe them well. Sprinkle them with salt and black pepper and roll each piece in flour, beaten eggs and cracker crumbs. Melt butter in a roster and then add the rabbit. Add the onion and cover. Roast the rabbit in an oven at 350°-375°) for 1½ hours. Baste the rabbit with hot water, using from 1 to 2 cups depending on amount of gravy desired. Continue to roast the rabbit, basting it frequently for ½ hour.

96. Venison Steak and Gravy

This is a terrific venison steak recipe. It calls for mushrooms and Mushroom sauce (see the recipe in Section IX.

Ingredients

4 venison steaks, ¼ pound each
1 cup of flour
Salt
Black pepper
4 tablespoons of lard
½ onion, chopped
6 fresh mushrooms, sliced
1 tablespoon of garlic, minced
Mushroom sauce
¼ cup milk

Directions

Cut all fat and gristle off the meat and pound each steak out with a meat tenderizer until it is thin but not tearing. Combine the flour, salt, and pepper in a shallow bowl. Dredge the steaks in the flour mixture until they are evenly coated. Heat 1 tablespoon of lard in a large iron skillet. Cook the onions until they are caramelized. Stir in the mushrooms, and garlic, and cook them until they are tender. Remove the mixture from the skillet and set it aside. Heat the remaining lard and fry each steak for 2 minutes on each side, or until it is golden brown. Return the onion mixture to skillet. Stir in the mushrooms and milk. Reduce the heat, cover, and simmer the steaks for 30-40 minutes. Stir the mixture occasionally to prevent it from sticking. When they are finished cooking pour the mushroom sauce over steaks and serve.

97. Country Fried Squirrel

Squirrels live in trees throughout the South. Their meat is lean, and it can be tough if ill-prepared. However, fried squirrel is a favorite among old-timers in the southern region.

Ingredients

2 or 3 squirrels, cut into sections
2 cups of buttermilk
2 eggs, beaten
Lard
2 cups of flour
2 teaspoons of garlic salt
2 teaspoons of paprika
1 tablespoon of salt
Black pepper

Directions

Mix the ingredients for the dredge in a shallow dish. Pat the squirrel dry, then dredge each piece in the seasoned flour. Move the coated squirrel to a wire rack. Save the remaining coating mixture. Mix the beaten eggs and buttermilk in a bowl or shallow dish. Dip the floured squirrel pieces, one at a time, into the egg wash. Heat 3" of lard in a heavy pot over medium-high heat. Once the shortening reaches 350° drop in the squirrel, a few pieces at a time. Don't overcrowd the pan. Fry the squirrel for 6 minutes until the coating is golden brown and crispy.

98. Groundhog Stew

Groundhog (aka woodchuck) is another dish that is less common in the South than it once was. Despite this, those that eat it swear that groundhog stew is a favorable and works well as a standalone dish or an early course in a larger meal.

Ingredients

1 groundhog (2-3 pound), quartered
Carrots, diced
Potatoes, diced
Onion, diced
Celery, diced
1 large tomato, chopped.
3 quarts of chicken broth
4 ounces of bacon, diced
Lard
½ tablespoon garlic, minced
1 cup of rice, cooked
1 ear of sweet corn
2 tablespoons of butter

Directions

Put the groundhog pieces in a large pan and brown them on medium high heat in the lard. Add the broth. Cover the pan and reduce the heat to a gentle simmer for 1½ hours. or until the meat can be picked from the bones. Cook the rice in the chicken broth until it is barely done, then strain out the rice and lay it out on a plate or cookie sheet to cool. Keep the rice liquid to add to the stew. Remove the groundhog pieces and let them cool, then pick the meat from the bones. Take the broth from the pan and strain it. Melt the butter and add the diced vegetables, bacon, and garlic. Cook the mixture for about 15 minutes until the ingredients are soft. Then add the groundhog liquid, tomato, rice liquid, and simmer it for 15 minutes more. Add the groundhog meat, corn, and rice. Season the stew with salt to taste.

99. Stuffed Opossum

The wild game section comes to a close with a recipe for stuffed opossum. "Possum" was once a very common dish in the South. Hunters and trappers were thrilled to bring an opossum for dinner. Today, it is rare for opossum to be on the dinner table, even in the most rural areas, but it is as much a part of the Southern heritage as is plowing with mules and tipping one's hat to his neighbor. The opossum is a very fat animal, with a peculiarly flavored meat that is definitely an acquired taste. This recipe employs opossum stuffing (see the recipe in Section IX). For instructions on how to dress a suckling pig see the recipe in Section I).

Ingredients

1 opossum
1 cup of salt
Water
Opossum stuffing

Directions

Dress the opossum as one would dress a suckling pig. Remove the opossum entrails, and if desired, the head and the tail. After it has been dressed, wash it thoroughly inside and outside with hot water. Cover it with cold water to which has been added 1 cup of salt. Allow it to stand overnight. The next morning, drain off the salted water and rinse the opossum well with clear, boiling water. Then cook the opossum as one would a roasted pig.

VIII. Eggs

Since chickens were found on most Southern homesteads, eggs were a part of Southern life as cuisine. They were also sold to earn a little cash.

Eggs are used as ingredients in countless recipes. Beyond that, there are hundreds of recipes that feature eggs. This little cookbook includes only 5 Southern egg recipes, but they are representative of the egg recipes created in the long ago South.

100. *Baked Egg Casserole*

Eggs make for great casseroles. This light casserole is made with eggs, cheese, and various vegetables baked together.

Ingredients

2½ cups of tomatoes
1 small onion, chopped
½ of a green pepper, chopped
1 teaspoon of sugar
1 cup of breadcrumbs
½ cup of celery
4 eggs
½ cup of American cheese, grated
Salt
Black pepper

Directions

Cook the tomatoes, pepper, onion, and the seasoning together for 10 minutes. Add the breadcrumbs and place the mixture in a casserole dish. Break the eggs on top and of the mixture and sprinkle it with salt and black pepper. Then cover it with grated cheese. Bake the mixture in an oven preheated to 350°. Continue baking the mixture until the eggs have set and the cheese has melted.

101. Hard Boiled Egg Casserole

This tangy and delightful casserole features eggs boiled hard and the always popular white sauce (see the recipe in Section IX). This particular casserole contains a bevy of veggies that will liven up any day.

Ingredients

6 eggs, boiled hard
2 cups of tomato juice
½ cup of chopped celery
¼ cup of green peppers, chopped
½ cup of mushrooms
1 tablespoon of flour
1 tablespoon of butter
½ onion, diced
½ teaspoon of Worcestershire sauce
½ cup of white sauce
Salt
Black pepper

Directions

Hard boil the eggs, then chop the egg whites and mash the yolks. Brown the onion in the butter, add the flour and blend well. Add the tomato juice and the green peppers and cook the mixture slowly until it is done. Add the mushrooms, the seasoning, and the Worcestershire sauce. When this is all done add the white sauce, the egg yolks, and the chopped egg whites. Place the mixture in a buttered casserole dish. Sprinkle the mixture with cracker crumbs, dot it with butter, and brown it in the oven. Serve it hot.

102. Eggs and White Sauce

This super simple egg dish is almost fool proof. It includes our old friend white sauce (see the recipe in Section IX) and toast.

Ingredients

3 eggs, boiled hard
1 cup of white sauce
6 slices of bread, toasted
parsley to garnish

Directions

Boil the eggs hard. Separate the yolks and whites of the eggs. Chop the egg whites finely and add them to the white sauce. Pour the white sauce over 4 pieces of toast. Mash the yolks through a strainer and sprinkle them over the top of the mixture. Cut the remaining toast into triangular shapes and place them on the side of the dish. Garnish the dish with parsley.

103. Eggs and Chicken Livers

This is a simple dish of eggs stuffed with chicken livers. It makes a fine side dish or appetizer. It employs tomato sauce (see the recipe in Section IX).

Ingredients

2 chicken livers
½ teaspoon of onion juice
2 tablespoons of butter
4 eggs, boiled hard
1 teaspoon of chopped parsley
Worcestershire sauce
¼ cup of grated cheese
Salt
Black pepper
Bread toasted
Tomato sauce

Directions

Clean the livers very thoroughly, chop them finely, and sprinkle them with onion juice. Fry the livers in butter. Cut the eggs in half, remove the yolks, and set the whites aside. Force the yolks through a sieve, add the parsley, salt, pepper, and Worcestershire sauce, and then mix with the chicken livers. Refill whites with the mixture, sprinkle with them grated cheese and bake until cheese melts. Serve with toast and a little tomato sauce.

104. Creole Sauce Omelet

Most omelets are fried with meat or vegetables. This simple omelet is comprised of just eggs and Creole sauce (see the recipe in Section IX).

Ingredients

1 tablespoon of butter
Water
4 eggs
Creole sauce

Directions

Beat the eggs in a bowl with four tablespoons of water. When the butter is heated to a light brown, add the eggs. As the eggs brown, lift the edges with a spatula, and make sure the omelet is brown underneath and creamy on top. Fold the omelet once and slip it onto a hot platter, surrounding it with Creole sauce.

IX. Complementary Dishes

Many of the meat dishes in this little volume are accompanied by sauces, stuffings, condiments, and other complimentary dishes. This section contains 27 such recipes. Some of these items can be readily interchanged with each other and some can be used as main dishes. Southerners were adept at adding complementary dishes to enhance the flavor of their meals and to increase otherwise skimpy portions during "hard times.".

105. Brown Gravy

Brown gravy virtually defines Southern cooking. It could be used when rations were short, or at any other time. Sometimes when times were tough a meal might have consisted of nothing more than brown gravy served over biscuits. This recipe calls for fried chicken drippings, but lard will work too, although the gravy won't taste as good.

Ingredients

½ cup of flour
¼ pound of butter
Fried chicken drippings
Water
Salt
Black pepper

Directions

Put butter in a medium size saucepan and heat it on medium. When the butter has melted, add the flour, salt, black pepper, and chicken drippings. Mix with a whisk and add enough water to get it to the correct texture (some may want their gravy a little thicker than others do). Let simmer it for 5 minutes and then serve.

106. White Gravy

One will notice that white gravy is similar in preparation to brown gravy. However, the taste is very different, and the uses vary.

Ingredients

2 tablespoons of fried chicken drippings
1 tablespoon of flour
1 cup of milk
Salt
Black pepper

Directions

In a saucepan, add 2 tablespoonfuls of fried chicken drippings, a tablespoon of flour, a little salt and black pepper, and a cup of milk, Bring the mixture to a boil, stirring them constantly. When the gravy is thick enough, serve it.

107. Chicken Sauce

Chicken sauce has many uses and may be used with a variety of dishes.

Ingredients

1½ cups of chicken broth
1 medium onion, sliced
2 tablespoons of celery, chopped
Salt
Black pepper
2 egg yolks
2 teaspoons of flour
1 tablespoon of butter
2 teaspoons of vinegar
2 teaspoons of parsley, chopped

Directions

Place the broth in saucepan with the onion, celery, salt, and black pepper and boil it for 4 minutes. Mix the egg yolks with the flour and when they are mixed well, add a tablespoon of broth, pour contents of the saucepan over the egg mixture very slowly, place on the stove and let it thicken, stirring it fast and evenly so that the sauce will not curdle. Add the butter, vinegar and parsley and stir until the butter melts. Strain the mixture into a gravy dish.

108. Corn Dodgers

Corn dodgers are an old Southern favorite. The are frequently served with pot likker. They are used with many other dishes too. After the Civil War when many Southerners migrated to the West, they took their corn dodger recipes along with them and corn dodgers became an Old West favorite too.

Ingredients

½ pound of white cornmeal
½ teaspoon of salt
2 tablespoons of butter
Water

Directions

Add salt to the cornmeal and stir in melted butter. Add sufficient cold water so the dough will hold its shape. Shape the dough into biscuit size pieces and drop it into a hot skillet and cook it until it is brown. Serve the corn dodgers on the side of the main course, or, as in the case of pot likker, within the main dish itself.

109. White Sauce

White sauce is very versatile and is an important part of many Southern dishes.

Ingredients

2 tablespoons of butter
2 tablespoons of flour
1½ cups of milk
½ teaspoon of salt

Directions

Melt the butter without browning it. Add the flour and salt and cook until the mixture is well blended. Add the milk slowly, stirring it constantly to keep it from scorching. When the sauce reaches the boiling point remove it from the heat and beat well, or until it is creamy.

110. Barbecue Sauce

Barbecue sauce is another food item identified closely with the South. This barbecue sauce will work with most any barbequed meat. It includes chili sauce (see the recipe in this Section).

Ingredients

¼ pound of butter
1 cup of vinegar
1 dill pickle, finely chopped
2 tablespoons of onion, chopped
2 tablespoons of Worcestershire sauce
2 tablespoons of chili sauce
4 slices of lemon
1 teaspoon of brown sugar
1 green pepper, finely chopped

Directions

Combine all the ingredients and mix them thoroughly. Place them in a saucepan and cook them on low heat until the butter melts, stirring constantly. Place the mixture in the top of a double boiler and keep it warm until ready for use on barbecued meats or as a sauce for barbecued sandwiches.

111. Shrimp Sauce

Shrimp sauce can be served with almost any kind of fish. This recipe includes white sauce (see the recipe in this Section).

Ingredients

1½ cups of cooked shrimp, chopped
3 tablespoons of lemon juice
1½ cups of white sauce
2 eggs, boiled hard
Parsley, minced

Directions

Soak the shrimp in the lemon juice for 30 minutes and then add it to the white sauce. When it is time to serve the shrimp sauce, add the finely chopped eggs and a little minced parsley and pour it over the fish dish.

112. Apple Ball Sauce

Apple ball sauce is a terrific and versatile condiment. This sauce works well with many dishes.

Ingredients

1 cup of sugar
1 cup of water
4 cloves
½ lemon peel, grated
1½ cups of apple balls

Directions

Make apple balls with a potato cutter. Make syrup with sugar and water. Add the lemon peel and the cloves. Cook the mixture for several minutes, then remove the lemon peel and the cloves. Drop in the apple balls. Cook it until the apples are done. Serve with poultry, roasts, or most other meat dishes.

113. Apple Stuffing

Apple stuffing adds a nice touch to several kinds of meat.

Ingredients

1 small onion
6 tablespoons of butter
1 cup of celery, chopped
3 cups of day old breadcrumbs
4 cups of apples, chopped
2 tablespoons of parsley, chopped
4 tablespoons of raisins
Salt
Black pepper

Directions

Chop the onion and brown it in the butter. Add the celery, breadcrumbs, apple, and parsley. Season it with salt and pepper and then add the raisins.

114. *Bread Stuffing*

Bread stuffing works great with any type of baked poultry. A variation of bread dressing can also be used with pork. Simply use pork liver and heart instead as chicken organs.

Ingredients

Day old bread, 1 loaf
1 teaspoon of salt
¼ teaspoon of black pepper
¼ teaspoon of poultry seasoning
1 teaspoon of parsley, chopped
½ teaspoon of onion, chopped fine
2 tablespoons of lard, melted
1 egg
Water
Chicken heart, liver, and gizzard, chopped finely

Directions

Soak 1 quart of day old bread in cold water and then squeeze it dry. Season the bread with 1 teaspoon of salt, ¼ teaspoon of black pepper, ¼ teaspoon of poultry seasoning, 1 teaspoon of chopped parsley, and ½ teaspoon of onion, chopped fine. Add 2 tablespoons of melted lard and mix it all thoroughly. Beat 1 egg lightly and add it to the above mixture. Then add the heart, liver and gizzard of the fowl chopped fine and partially boiled.

115. Mushroom Sauce

Mushroom sauce may have come to the Southland from Germany where it is used in pork schnitzel. Regardless of its origin, mushroom sauce is great with poultry and beef.

Ingredients

1 medium sized can of mushrooms
4 tablespoons of butter
3 tablespoons of flour
1 cup of cream

Directions

Sauté the mushrooms in the butter. Add the flour slowly and brown the mixture slightly. Add the cream and cook the mixture until it thickens. Pour the sauce over steak or chicken.

116. Chestnut Stuffing

It is traditional to bake Christmas turkey or New Year's goose with chestnut stuffing. Of course, it is good anytime.

Ingredients

1 egg
1 pound of chestnuts
¼ cup of lard
¼ cup of butter
2 cups of celery, chopped
½ cup of onions, chopped
6 cups of breadcrumbs
Parsley, chopped fine
Salt
Black pepper

Directions

Boil the chestnuts for about twenty minutes. Remove the shells and brown their skins while the nuts are still hot. Melt the lard and add the butter. Cook the celery and the onion in this for 3-5 minutes. Add a few sprigs of chopped parsley, the egg, breadcrumbs, and chestnuts. Season to taste with salt and black pepper. Stir the mixture until it is thoroughly hot. Wipe the chicken or turkey dry inside, sprinkle it with salt, and fill it with hot stuffing.

117. Tomato Sauce

This old southern recipe for delicious tomato sauce is very good for veal cutlets, fish, and other meats as well as for a variety of vegetable dishes. Try it with your favorite rice dish or macaroni casserole.

Ingredients

3 tablespoons of butter
3 tablespoons of flour
1 cup of canned tomatoes
1 tablespoon of sugar
¼ teaspoon of cloves
½ teaspoon of allspice
Salt
Black pepper

Directions

Melt the butter without browning it. Add the flour and the salt and cook it until it is well blended. Add the tomatoes slowly, stirring the mixture constantly to prevent scorching. When the mixture reaches the boiling point remove it from the heat and beat it until it is creamy.

118. Shrimp Sauce

Shrimp sauce is a welcome addition to one's favorite seafood dish. It can be served with almost any kind of fish. White sauce (see the recipe in this Section).

Ingredients

1½ cups of cooked shrimp, chopped
3 tablespoons of lemon juice
1½ cups of white sauce
2 eggs, boiled hard
Parsley, minced

Directions

Boil the eggs. Soak the shrimp in the lemon juice for ½ hour and add them to the white sauce. When it is ready to serve, add the finely chopped eggs and a little minced parsley. Pour this over the fish.

119. Opossum Stuffing

"Possum" has its own stuffing. Additionally, this stuffing can be adjusted to use with other meats.

Ingredients

Opossum liver, finely chopped
1 tablespoon of butter
1 large onion, finely chopped
1 cup of breadcrumbs
Red pepper, chopped
Worcestershire sauce
1 egg, boiled hard and finely chopped
Salt
Water

Directions

Melt 1 tablespoon of butter in a frying pan and add 1 large finely chopped onion. When the onion begins to brown, add the finely chopped opossum liver. Cook it until the liver is tender and well done. Add 1 cup of breadcrumbs, a little chopped red pepper, a dash of Worcestershire sauce, 1 finely chopped egg, boiled hard, salt and water to moisten. Stuff the opossum with the mixture.

120. Pie Dough

Pie dough is extremely easy to make. Using the homemade variety gives a dish a distinctive Southern flavor – literally and figuratively.

Ingredients

2 cups of flour
½ teaspoon of salt
1 cup of butter or lard
1/2 cup of ice water

Directions

Mix the flour and salt. Work the butter lightly into the flour. Add the ice water and mix the ingredients to make a stiff dough, but do not knead the dough. Roll the dough and line the pie plate with it.

121. Southern Cornbread

There is nothing more Southern than "good ole" cornbread. Cornbread can be served with meat courses, soups, stews. It will work with virtually any dish mentioned in this book.

Ingredients

1 cup of white cornmeal
¼ cup of wheat flour
1 teaspoon baking powder
½ teaspoon of salt
1 egg, beaten
½ cup of milk
1 tablespoon of butter, melted

Directions

Sift the dry ingredients together. Combine the milk with the egg and add it to the dry ingredients. Add the melted butter and pour the batter into a well-greased pan. Bake the mixture for about 25 minutes in a preheated oven at 425°.

122. Baked Oranges

Baked oranges may be served with any of several poultry dishes.

Ingredients

4 seedless oranges, boiled
2 cups of sugar
1 cup of the orange water
Butter

Directions

Wash the oranges and place them in a large pot. Pour boiling water over them. Cook them until they are tender. Remove the oranges from the water, cut them in half and arrange them in a baking dish. Cook the sugar and orange water together for 5 minutes. Pour the sugared orange water over the oranges and dot each orange with a piece of butter. Cover the baking dish and bake the oranges in a preheated oven for about ½ hour or until the oranges become transparent.

123. Guava Jelly

Guava fruit comes is a tree of the same name that grows in Central and South America. It has been popular in the American South and Southwest for generations. Guava jelly is tasty and works great as a sauce. It is also easy to prepare.

Ingredients

1 pound of guavas
1 pound of sugar
1 quart of water

Directions

Wash the guavas well. Remove the blossom end and slice. For each pound of fruit, add 2 pints of water and cook the guavas until they are soft. Let the guavas stand until they are cold. Strain out the juice. Add one measure of sugar for one measure of fruit. Bring the juice to a boil and add the sugar. Continue to boil the fruit to the jellying point.

124. *Frozen Mint Ice*

Frozen mint can perk up any number of dishes, especially lamb. Food coloring is not necessary to this recipe, but most people want anything mint to be green.

Ingredients

Fresh mint
½ cup of lemon juice
½ cup of confectioner's sugar
4 cups of water
¼ teaspoon of peppermint extract essence
Green food coloring

Directions

Wash and pick mint from the stems and soak it in lemon juice for ½ hour, then strain it. Dissolve ½ cup of sugar in 4 cups of water and it add to the strained lemon and mint juice. Just before freezing it, add the green food coloring and peppermint extract. Freeze it until it is slushy.

125. Raisin Sauce

Rasin sauce isn't as common as some other Southern sauces, but it is a good tasting sauce, nonetheless.

Ingredients

1 cup of raisins
1 cup of water
5 cloves
¾ cup of brown sugar
1 teaspoon of cornstarch
¼ teaspoon of salt
Black pepper
1 tablespoon of butter
1 tablespoon of vinegar
¼ teaspoon of Worcestershire sauce

Directions

Cover the raisins with water. Add the cloves and simmer them with the raisins for about 10 minutes. Mix the sugar, cornstarch, salt, and black pepper together and add it to the raisins and cloves. Stir the mixture until it is slightly thickened. Then add the remaining ingredients.

126. Hush Puppies

Catfish without hushpuppies? Unthinkable. Hush puppies are as Southern as hound dogs barking on a cool autumn evening. This hush puppy recipe makes for a pleasing side dish of Southern goodness.

Ingredients

2 cups of yellow corn meal
2 teaspoons of baking powder
Lard
1 teaspoon of salt
1½ cups of milk
½ cup of water
1 large onion, chopped fine
Catfish crumbs

Directions

Sift the dry ingredients together and add the milk and water. Stir in the chopped onion and crumbs from the catfish. Add more meal or milk as may be necessary to form a soft but workable dough. Mold pieces of the dough into pones (oblong cakes, about 5 inches long and 3 inches wide, and about ¼ of an inch thick). Deep fry the hush puppies until they are golden brown.

127. Cornbread Dressing

Cornbread dressing is a terrific dish that serves its purpose very well.

Ingredients

3 eggs, beaten
2 cups of buttermilk
3 tablespoons of lard, melted
2 teaspoons of salt
2½ cups of sifted yellow cornmeal
3 teaspoons of baking powder
1 teaspoon of baking soda
1 tablespoon of water
3 tablespoons of butter, melted
Onion
Parsley
Celery
Salt
Black pepper

Directions

Add the well beaten eggs milk, lard, and salt together. Sift the baking powder and cornmeal together stir it slowly into the egg mixture, adding enough of the meal to make a medium thick batter. Beat well the batter well. Dissolve the baking soda in 1 tablespoon of water and add it to the batter. Pour the batter into a greased baking pan. Bake the batter in an oven preheated to 425° for 20-25 minutes, or until the bread begins to brown. Allow the bread to cool then crumble it into small pieces. Add the melted butter and season it with onion, celery, salt, and pepper. Then moisten it with hot water.

128. French Dressing

In the old days, Southerners didn't rush out to the market every time they needed a little dressing to pour across a dish. They made it themselves. This is certainly a French dressing recipe, but it is likely different in texture and taste from any other French dressing you have ever used. Still, it is very good, especially for fish dishes.

Ingredients

4 tablespoons of olive oil
1 clove of garlic
1¼ tablespoons of vinegar
¼ teaspoon of salt
¼ teaspoon of white pepper

Directions

Soak the garlic in the olive oil. Then remove the garlic before using the oil. Discard the garlic. Mix the salt and the white pepper together. Add some olive oil and stir it together with the salt and pepper. Add the vinegar and the remaining oil and mix everything together well.

129. French Bread

Today, if we need a loaf of French bread, we jump in the car, drive to the market, and pick up one. In times past, many Southerners wouldn't make the trip into town more than a couple times a year. If they wanted French bread, they had to make it themselves with ingredients stored in their pantries. Here is a great made from scratch French bread recipe that will satisfy even the most discriminating taste.

Ingredients

1 tablespoon of cornmeal
6 cups of flour
2 tablespoons of dry yeast
1½ teaspoons of salt
2 cups of water warmed to 110°
1 egg white
1 tablespoon of water

Directions

Grease a large baking sheet and sprinkle it with cornmeal. Set it aside. Combine 2 cups of flour, the yeast, and the salt in a mixing bowl. Stir in 2 cups of warm water. Beat ingredients until they are blended. Continue adding flour, a little at a time, until it is all mixed in. Knead the dough on a lightly floured surface for 8-10 minutes until it is smooth and elastic. Shape the dough into a ball, place it in a greased bowl, and turn it once to get it evenly greased. Cover the dough and put it in a warm place for about 1 hour until it has risen to twice it previous size. Punch the dough down and divide it in half. Turn it out onto a lightly floured surface. Cover it and let it rest for 10 minutes. Roll each half of the dough into a large rectangle. Roll up it, starting from a long side. Moisten the edge of the dough with water and seal it. Taper its ends. Place the loaves, seam side down, on the prepared baking sheet. Lightly beat the egg white with 1 tablespoon of water and brush the egg white over the loaves. Cover the loaves with a damp cloth and let them rise for 35-40 minutes until they are nearly doubled in size. Preheat an oven to 375°. Use a sharp knife to make 3 or 4 diagonal cuts, about ¼" deep, across the top of each loaf. Bake the loaves in the oven for 20 minutes. Brush the loaves with egg white mixture. Continue baking the loaves for 15-20 minutes or until they sound hollow when tapped. Remove the loaves from the baking sheet and cool them on a wire rack.

130. Chili Sauce

Chili sauce can be used in several ways. The homemade variety is superior to all others. It is one of the easiest condiments to make too.

Ingredients

1 cup of tomato sauce
¼ cup of brown sugar
2 tablespoons of vinegar
¼ teaspoon of allspice

Directions

Stir the tomato sauce, brown sugar, vinegar, and allspice together in a mixing bowl until they are thoroughly blended. Pour the mixture into a covered container and refrigerate it until ready to use.

131. Creole Sauce

Creole sauce is a major ingredient in the omelet that includes its name (see page xxx), but it can be used in many other dishes as well.

Ingredients

2 tablespoons of olive oil
2 onions
4 tomatoes
2 green peppers
1 teaspoon of salt
½ teaspoon of paprika

Directions

Heat two tablespoons of olive oil. Add the onions, tomatoes, and peppers to it. Then add the salt and paprika. Cook the mixture slowly until it is needed for the omelet.

From the Author

I hope that you found this book interesting and useful and that you have enjoyed reading it as much as I did writing it. I also hope you will refer to it often while you are cooking up some grub.

Again, I say, bon appétit, y'all.

About the Author

CL Gammon has had a life-long fascination with the written word. This fascination has led to his authoring more than sixty books. Gammon studied Political Science at Tennessee Technological University and History and Government at Hillsdale College. He has received prestigious honors including the Certificate of Appreciation for Service to the State of Tennessee, the Partisan Prohibition Historical Society Citation of Merit (the only two-time recipient), and nomination for the 2023 Gilder Lehrman Lincoln Prize. Colleges, including the State University of New York and the University of Akron, have utilized his books as course material. Articles written by Gammon have appeared in more than a dozen national and regional publications. He has also written feature articles for his hometown newspaper, *The Macon County Times*. Gammon lives in Lafayette, Tennessee.

www.ingramcontent.com/pod-product-compliance
Lightning Source LLC
Chambersburg PA
CBHW060753050426
42449CB00008B/1388